THE
DISCERNING
TRAVELER'S
GUIDE TO
ROMANTIC
HIDEAWAYS
OF
NEW ENGLAND

*The Discerning Traveler's Guide
to the Middle Atlantic States*

The Discerning Traveler's Guide to New England

*The Discerning Traveler's Guide
to Romantic Hideaways of the Middle Atlantic and
South Eastern States*

Visit our website at www.discerningtraveler.com

THE

DISCERNING TRAVELER'S GUIDE TO ROMANTIC HIDEAWAYS OF NEW ENGLAND

DAVID AND LINDA GLICKSTEIN

Maps by David Glickstein

ST. MARTIN'S GRIFFIN
NEW YORK

Maps by David Glickstein
Design by Chris Welch

ISBN 0-312-19858-2

First St. Martin's Griffin Edition: February 1999

10 9 8 7 6 5 4 3 2 1

In memory of Nancy Glickstein

CONTENTS

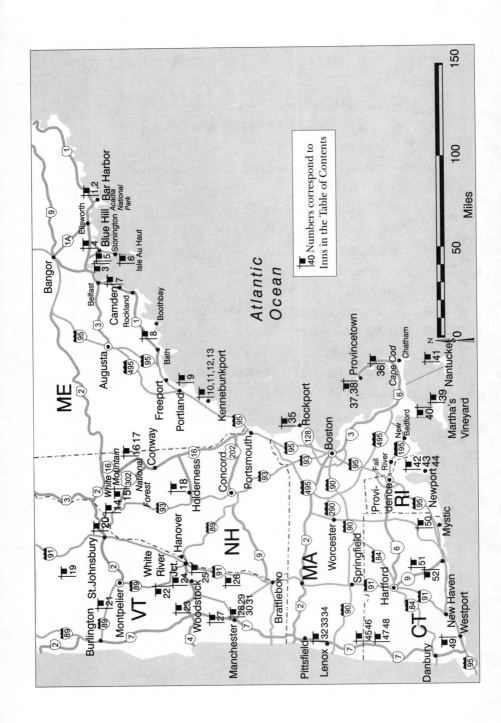

INTRODUCTION

Close your eyes and imagine your ideal romantic hideaway. To some, this means a small inn, warm and cozy, with a working fireplace, crisp linens, plush pillows, and a canopy bed. To others, it is formal elegance with expansive rooms, a panoramic view of mountains, and formal dining. Some see a quiet porch with rocking chairs and a view of a colorful sunset over water; others relish sleeping late, luxuriating in a whirlpool tub, and enjoying a gourmet breakfast served in front of a fireplace. You might find the excitement of a city at your doorstep enticing, or you might prefer a remote location with more rustic facilities and the undeveloped splendor of thick forests and untouched shorelines.

A truly great inn, hotel, or resort is not just a package of amenities, a list of ingredients mixed and spread in certain proportions. Each place in this book has intangible as well as tangible aspects that create a unique experience. At its best, innkeeping is a commitment, an ideal, a striving for perfection. Many of the hostelries we describe are virtual museums of treasured antiques and artifacts, the result of years of passionate collecting.

Sharing a few days with someone special is time and money well spent. The gifts of time, love, and caring are some of the most meaningful gifts you can give. An experience that you and your loved one have shared can never be taken away from you.

That is what this book is all about: a gift of romantic hideaways where you can create lasting memories.

Each of these hideaways has its own distinctive features. From fairy-tale houses and charming cottages to elegant grand hotels, all have picturesque settings that are sure to nurture the soul. No matter where you live or when you plan to travel, you're sure to find that special haven, that romantic hideaway right for you.

Listings are arranged by state, starting with the northernmost destination in Maine and ending with southern Connecticut. The map shows the approximate location of each. The rates listed are for two persons per night, based on double occupancy. If there is a service charge, we list it, but state and local lodging taxes are additional.

Helping you choose a place to stay, and select the room that best suits your taste, is our first consideration. We've also included short sections on where to dine, what to do in the area, and how to get to each of these hideaways.

All of the places that we have selected were reviewed in issues of our newsletter, "The Discerning Traveler",® based on our personal visits. The choice of inns was ours alone; no one has paid to be included in this book. Further information about the areas in which each of these inns, bed-and-breakfasts, and hotels are located can be found in issues of "The Discerning Traveler"® and two guidebooks, *The Discerning Traveler's Guide to New England* and *The Discerning Traveler's Guide to the Middle Atlantic States*.

We have made every attempt to verify prices at the time this book went to press. It always is wise to call ahead, however, as many of the inns and restaurants are small and subject to changes in management, prices, and policies.

Finding romantic hideaways is a continuing process. We welcome your suggestions of other romantic hideaways. Please send your thoughts to us at 504 West Mermaid Lane, Philadelphia, Pennsylvania 19118.

Happy travels,
David and Linda Glickstein

THE DISCERNING TRAVELER'S GUIDE TO ROMANTIC HIDEAWAYS OF NEW ENGLAND

The Inn at Canoe Point

The Inn at Canoe Point, *Bar Harbor, Maine*

Tucked into a quiet cove on the rocky Maine coast, the Inn at Canoe Point offers spacious rooms, picture windows, wood-burning fireplaces in the common rooms, and gourmet breakfasts. To get there, turn off the main road leading into Bar Harbor onto a narrow gravel drive that winds through a stately grove of evergreens.

Dominating the first floor of this century-old Tudor-style home is the ocean room, with floor-to-ceiling windows overlooking Frenchman Bay. In summer breakfast is served on the wide deck that wraps around the room. In colder weather a favorite spot is the sectional sofa set in front of the granite fireplace. Two easy chairs with a pair of binoculars within reach are ideal for armchair birders. Placed about the room are plants and flowers and a dish filled with chocolate candy kisses. Delve into the extensive library upstairs for a good book or a few magazines and you won't want to leave the inn until dinnertime.

The entry hall living room is a second common room with a tuned baby grand piano, a sofa, and a wood-burning granite corner fireplace.

The most romantic room is the large Master Suite, with a late-nineteenth-century chaise longue and two easy chairs set by the gas fireplace. You'll have a wonderful view of the water from the queen-size bed. A deck with lounge chairs is shared with the adjoining Anchor Room, which is smaller than the Master Suite.

The secluded third-floor Garret Suite has two separate rooms, one with a king-size bed and the other furnished as a sitting room. Three windows situated directly in front of the king-size bed give a clear view of the water. The main attraction of this suite, however, is that you have the entire third floor as your private domain.

For romance on a more moderate budget, pick the smallest room in the house, the Garden Room, which gives the illusion of being the largest. Windows on three sides let you hear and see the ocean and feel as though your toes are practically in the water. The queen-size bed is nestled in a white railing. Down a step, a sitting area is furnished with a white wicker settee and rocker. Off the sitting area is your own private entrance, which leads directly to the rocky shore.

In the rooms, thick terry robes, a decanter of port (except for the Port-Side Room, where the brown decor coordinates better with a decanter of sherry), and cocktail napkins embossed with the room's name are thoughtful touches.

At breakfast, the combination of good food and a spectacular setting encourages lengthy conversations with innkeepers and owners Nancy and Tom Cervelli and other guests. What better way to start the day than with a glass of fresh orange juice followed by fresh fruit, a hot entrée such as omelettes with a choice of filling, eggs Benedict, or fluffy apple or blueberry pancakes?

Five rooms, each with private bath. Memorial Day through October, $150–$245; other times of the year, $80–$150. Full breakfast included. Children over 16 welcome. Rooms are double occupancy only. No pets. No smoking. Box 216, Hulls Cove, ME 04644; (207) 288-9511; fax (207) 288-2870; www. innatcanoepoint.com.

Where to Dine. During the season, we suggest Redfield's (in Northeast Harbour; (207) 276-5283), George's (7 Stephens Lane; (207) 288-4505) and the Porcupine Grill (123 Cottage Street; (207) 288-3884), both in Bar Harbor. The Burning Tree, in Otter Creek, has excellent seafood (207) 288-9331). The Jordan Pond House, on the Loop Road in Acadia National Park (207) 276-3316, has a pretty setting and is open for lunch, tea, and dinner.

What to Do. Hiking, canoeing, and swimming can all be enjoyed in Acadia National Park during the summer. Take the Loop Road through the park to Thunder Hole, Cadillac Mountain (a hike to its summit at dawn is a popular pilgrimage for those who want to be the first on the East Coast to see the sunrise), and the Jordan Pond House for tea and popovers. In Northeast Harbor, stop at the Asticou Azalea Garden—a Japanese strolling garden—and the Thuya Lodge and Gardens. Take a side trip to Schoodic Point, about 40 miles to the north, where the rugged beauty of the coast and the waves are particularly impressive. In winter the carriage trails are groomed for cross-country skiing, and Echo Lake is cleared for skating.

How to Get There. Fly into Bangor or take I-95 to Bangor. Then take Route 1A south to Ellsworth and Route 3 south toward Bar Harbor. The inn is located off Route 3, just beyond the entrance to Acadia National Park.

View of Frenchman's Bay from the Sun Porch of the Inn at Bay Ledge

The Inn at Bay Ledge, *Bar Harbor, Maine*

The inn, located off Route 3.5 mile down a quiet road about 7 miles north of the center of Bar Harbor, is in a tranquil setting perched on a ledge eighty feet above Frenchman Bay. From the inn you walk down a wooden staircase that hugs the cliff to a secluded rocky beach. Cavelike shelters called the Ovens and Cathedral Rock, a massive rock formation with an opening you can walk through, are natural features unique to this property, owned by innkeepers Jack and Jeani Ochtera.

The first floor has pine walls, two wood-burning fireplaces with comfortable seating, and French doors opening onto a wide deck overlooking the water. They have added an enclosed sun room off the living room, where breakfast is served. A few steps from the deck is a good-sized heated outdoor pool with a view of the bay. And, unless you are afraid of heights, be sure to spend some time sitting in the two chairs at the edge of the ledge, with an amazing view of the water.

The large sauna and steam shower on the first floor are popular, especially after a day of hiking in Acadia National Park. The second-floor hall sitting room has a television and a VCR.

Jeani has a flair for decorating. Fabrics used for draperies and comforters carry designer names such as Ralph Lauren, Brunswig and Fils, and Schumaker. The beds are made with damask sheets, a feather bed, and down comforters. You can see the water from all of the rooms in the main building except one.

Our favorite rooms are on the second floor, with a full front view of Frenchman Bay. Room 7 is the largest room, with a high four-poster carved king-size canopy bed, camelback couch, wingback chair, and bath with a whirlpool tub. Room 8 has an antique oak king-size bed, 1789 rattan oak baby carriage, pair of comfortable down wingback chairs, and bath with a whirlpool tub. Room 9, a smaller room with a queen-size canopy bed, is Jeani's favorite as it has a view of the water with Schoodic Mountain as the backdrop. Room 10, the most secluded, has a queen-size canopy bed and water views from a small deck. Room 4, on the first floor, has a queen-size bed with a view of Schoodic Mountain. Room 6, the lowest-priced water-view room, is a small room with an iron queen-size bed and bay window seat. Room 11, the only room in the inn with no water view, has a private entrance and deck that looks into the woods.

There are also three attached cottages across the road in a wooded setting with no water view. Our preference is Cottage 1, as it has a fieldstone fireplace and king-size bed. The other two cottages do not have fireplaces. Cottage 2 has a queen-size canopy bed, and Cottage 3 has a queen-size bed as well as a daybed. The cottages have a country decor with wicker furniture and baths with showers only. They offer a lot of privacy.

Breakfast, served from 8 to 9 A.M. in the new sun room,

includes juice; a fruit plate; granola made with cranberries and cashews; muffins, breads, or pastry; and a hot dish such as a tart filled with mascarpone cheese and fruits; Bay Ledge hash, made with layers of hashed browns, turkey, and three types of cheese; or Belgian waffles with different sauces. In the afternoon they serve lemonade slush and cookies. They also have beer and wines for purchase and like to feature local fruit wines from Bartlett Vineyards.

Open May through mid-October. Seven rooms and three cottages. Mid-June through mid-October, rooms $150–$250, cottages $135–$155; May to mid-June, rooms $85–$150, cottages $85–$100. Breakfast and afternoon refreshment included. Not appropriate for children under 16; third person in two of the cottages $25. No pets. No smoking. Two-night minimum in season. 1385 Sand Point Road, Bar Harbor, ME 04609; (207) 288-4204; fax (207) 288-5573; www.maine guide.com/barharbor/bayledge.

Where to Dine. Our favorite restaurants in Bar Harbor are the Porcupine Grill (123 Cottage Street, (207) 288-3884) and George's (7 Stephens Lane, (207) 288-4505). In Seal Harbor, we like the Bistro (Route 3, (207) 276-3299). Redfields (Main Street, Northeast Harbor; (207) 276-5283) is the best restaurant in the area. For lobster and great sunset views, go to Abel's Lobster Pound on Somes Sound (Route 198; (207) 276-5827). The Jordan Pond House (on the Loop Road in Acadia National Park; (207) 276-3316) has a pretty setting and is a good choice for lunch or tea.

What to Do. Hiking, horseback riding, bicycling, canoeing, and swimming can all be enjoyed in Acadia National Park during the summer. Take the Loop Road through the park to Thunder Hole, Cadillac Mountain (a hike to its summit at dawn is a popular pilgrimage for those who want to be the first on the East Coast to see the sunrise), and to the Jordan Pond House for tea and popovers. In Northeast Harbor, stop at the Asticou Azalea Garden—a Japanese strolling garden—and the Thuya Lodge and Gardens. The Rockefeller Gardens, in Seal Harbor, are now open once a week in the summer by reservation.

How to Get There. Fly into Bangor or take I-95 to Bangor. Take Route 1A south to Ellsworth and Route 3 south to Mount Desert Island, approximately 7 miles. Turn left on Sand Point Road and continue .5 mile to the inn.

View of Penobscot Bay from the porch at Eggemoggin Reach Bed and Breakfast

Eggemoggin Reach Bed and Breakfast,
Brooksville, Maine

The inn, located on a secluded rugged granite cove with a spectacular view of Eggemoggin Reach, Pumpkin Island Lighthouse, Penobscot Bay, and in the distance the outline of the Camden Hills, is a perfect hideaway for those who crave the seclusion of picture-book Maine coast. One would never find this inn without directions, as it is down a long entrance drive off a back road. Innkeepers Susie and Mike Canon originally built the house as a summer home in 1989 and turned it into a bed-and-breakfast in 1993. A wooden staircase leads from the house down to the dock and the rocky shoreline, where there are a rowboat and a canoe for the guests' use.

The first floor of the inn is an open plan with no doors separating the dining, living, and kitchen areas. A porch that faces west for dramatic sunset views over the water is where breakfast is served. The living room has comfortable seating, a good selection of books, satellite television, and a wood-burning fireplace.

The Wheelhouse Suite in the main house, the studio cottages, and Tuckaway Cottage all have excellent water views.

Tuckaway Cottage, located 275 feet from the main house, is the most private accommodation. A winding staircase leads from the ground-floor entrance to a large living room about 20 feet square with a 16 foot cathedral ceiling, woodstove, satellite television, phone, and a fully equipped kitchen with granite countertops. The bedroom has a queen-size bed. A deck off the living room and a much larger deck on the first floor, both with great views, make this an ideal choice for someone who wants to do some cooking and wants a lot of space.

The two attached cottage units a few steps from the main inn are also very private. Each pickled pine, cathedral ceiling studio has a king-size bed, fireplace stove, couch, fully equipped small kitchen, screened porch, and bath with a shower only. We like Starboard Watch, which has a more expansive water view than Port Watch.

A new building tucked into the woods has two rooms on each of three levels, all with great water views. Each has a kitchen, king-size bed (one can be made into two twin beds), and large screened porch or outdoor sitting area directly facing the water. Bradbury and Fiddlehead are on the top level, with superb views. Pickering and Spruce are on the middle level, similar except each has a woodstove. Pumpkin and Vinalhaven are on the ground level.

The Wheelhouse Suite, the entire third floor of the main house, has a bedroom with a king-size bed, full bath, and a very large living room with a desk, couch, and two twin beds tucked into the eaves.

A breakfast buffet includes fresh squeezed orange juice, cereals, yogurt, fruit, muffins, and a hot dish such as waffles, apple-cinnamon French toast, or sausage-and-egg casserole.

Open May through mid-October. Ten rooms, each with private bath, $150–$175. Breakfast included. Children over 12 welcome. Third person $48 additional. No pets. No smoking. Two-night weekend minimum. RR1, Box 33A, Herrick Road, Brooksville, ME 04617; (207) 359-5073, (888) 625-8866; fax (207) 359-5074.

Where to Dine. For lobster-in-the-rough go to Eaton's Lobster Pool Restaurant on Little Deer Isle (207) 348-2383) or to Eaton's Pier in Sunshine (207) 348-2489), where you sit at picnic tables. For fine dining close to the inn go to the Landing in Bucks Harbor, South Brooksville (207) 326-8483). In Blue Hill two good choices are Firepond (207) 374-9970), with the prize tables next to a rushing stream, or Jonathan's (207) 374-5226). Three close inns that welcome outside guests for dinner on a space-available basis (reservations only) are Pilgrim's Inn in Deer Isle (207) 348-6615), Goose Cove Lodge in Sunset (207) 348-2508), and Blue Hill Inn in Blue Hill (207) 374-2844).

What to Do. This is a major crafts area. Visit Blue Hill, Deer Isle, and Stonington. Rowantrees and Rackliffe potteries and Leighton Gallery for contemporary paintings and sculpture are in Blue Hill. Stop in at the Maine Crafts Association in Deer Isle for information on over 100 craftspeople. Don't miss Blue Heron Gallery in Deer Isle for some of the finest crafts by teachers at the renowned Haystack Mountain School of Crafts (tour Wednesday afternoon). Poke through the many galleries in the fishing village of Stonington. Walk along the waterfront in Castine. Take a day sail on Penobscot Bay with Gil Perkins, go kayaking, or head to Bar Harbor and Acadia National Park, about an hour's drive, for spectacular ocean and mountain scenery. There are miles of magnificent hiking and walking trails through the park. Stop at the visitors center in Hulls Cove for information about daily ranger-led walks, hikes, and naturalist-led boat trips. Plan ahead during summer months and get a reservation to visit the Rockefeller Garden in Seal Harbor on Thursdays. Stroll around the wealthy summer community of Northeast Harbor and visit the Asticou Azalea Garden and the Thuya Lodge and Gardens.

How to Get There.   Take I-95 north to Augusta; Route 3 to Belfast; Route 1 through Bucksport to Route 15 south to Blue Hill. Continue on Route 15 for 4.5 miles; take a left at a "T" and continue for 2.9 miles to the intersection with Route 175. Turn right on Route 175 (follow sign to Brooksville) for .5 mile. Bear left at Route 176 for .9 mile. Turn left at Herrick Road and continue for 1.8 miles to Eggemoggin Reach Bed-and-Breakfast.

The Blue Hill Inn

The Blue Hill Inn, *Blue Hill, Maine*

Opening the front door of this traditional brick and white clapboard 1830s New England village inn on a chilly fall afternoon to the sight of a fireplace and couches invitingly set on either side and the warm greeting of innkeepers Mary and Don Hartley, we felt right at home. The tastefully coordinated rooms vary in size from enormous to comfortable. Many have yellow pine floors original to the house and nineteenth-century antiques.

If reading in bed and watching a wood-burning fire after a delicious dinner fit your image of a romantic New England inn, choose Room 5, a second-floor corner room with a queen-size four-poster cannonball bed; Room 10, a first-floor corner room with a fireplace and a queen-size bed; or Room 4, with a king-size bed, a fireplace, and an old-fashioned clawfoot tub. Room 8, the most popular room in the summer, is the longest room, with a king-size four-poster bed and windows on three sides of the room overlooking the perennial garden. Room 3 is also very popular, as it has a queen-size bed, large sitting area, and bath with a clawfoot tub. Room 9, a third-floor room with a bath between the bedroom and the sitting room, is the only room that can accommodate three people.

The Cape House, next door, is a large luxury suite with a cathedral ceiling, a king-size canopy bed, a raised-hearth wood-burning fireplace, and a sitting area with a pull-out couch, television, and phone. The suite (which is handicap-accessible) has a marble-tiled bath, a full kitchen (including an espresso machine), and an outdoor deck with a Weber grill.

Breakfast includes freshly squeezed orange juice, muffins, and fruit, plus a choice of five entrées such as amaretto French toast, waffles with strawberries, olive-and-chive ome-lettes, or blueberry pancakes.

Guests begin to gather either in the parlor with a wood-burning fireplace or outside in the garden starting at 6 P.M. The innkeepers, both quite knowledgeable about wines, help their guests select a wine before dinner so it can be opened and ready at their table when they sit down at 7. There are copies of the wine list in each guest room.

A leisurely five-course dinner with a choice of two entrées is served to a maximum of twenty-four guests, all at individual tables. The dining room has a candlelit chandelier. Tables are set with white linen and a single candle on each table. The inn features locally raised produce, fowl, and Maine seafood.

Dinner starts with an appetizer such as leeks in puff pastry with a chervil sauce; fettuccine with lobster, arugula, and fresh tomatoes; or mussels Provençal. This is followed by a palate-cleansing ice. A choice of two entrées could include Spinney Creek oysters in a curry sauce, roasted herb-stuffed loin of lamb, filet of beef with Roquefort sauce and walnuts, scallops with endive and lime, guinea hen with champagne grapes and wild mushrooms, and lobster with caramelized ginger served on a bed of spinach. The salad—watercress and walnuts or mixed native greens with a balsamic vinaigrette—follows the entrée. Coffee and a dessert such as a flourless chocolate torte or poached pears in red wine and cassis complete the meal.

Three times a year in the spring and fall a seven-course wine dinner with five wines is served as a special event at the inn. We went to a September wine dinner, a highlight of our trip; were introduced to a variety of new wines, all of which are available at a local wine store; and met a number of guests who have the good sense to plan their yearly vacations to coincide with these dinners.

Outside diners should call far in advance for reservations as only a few non-guests can be accommodated.

Open mid-May through November. Eleven rooms and the Cape House Suite, each with private bath. June to mid-October $150–$190, Cape House, $200–$260, includes breakfast and dinner for two. Other times $100–$130, Cape House $190, breakfast included. Bed-and-breakfast rates available. 15% service charge. Dinner served June through mid-October, Wednesday through Sunday (Tuesday also in July). Dinner for guests not staying at the inn (reservations only) $30 per person, not including tax, gratuity, and drinks. Innkeepers' reception at 6 P.M., dinner at 7 P.M. Children over 13 welcome in the inn, younger children welcome in the Cape House. No pets. No smoking. Two-night weekend and holiday minimum. Union Street, Box 403, Blue Hill, ME 04614; (207) 374-2844, (800) 826-7415; fax (207) 374-2829; www.bluehillinn.com.

What to Do. Communities to visit on the peninsula include Blue Hill, Castine, Deer Isle, and Stonington, all of which have many galleries, antiques shops, and craft stores. This is a major crafts area. On Deer Isle, the well-known Hay-

stack Mountain School of Crafts and the Wooden Boat School
are open in the summer only; call to find out visiting hours.
Be sure to visit the Blue Heron Gallery in Deer Isle, a top craft
gallery. In Blue Hill, visit two pottery factories, Rowantrees
and Rackliffe; the Leighton Gallery is one of the top galleries
in Maine.

Take a day's sail from Stonington, Castine, or Brooksville;
take the mailboat to Isle au Haut and walk the trails; or hike
to the top of Blue Hill Mountain. During the summer, attend
the Kneisel Hall chamber music concerts. The Left Bank Café,
a good choice for lunch, holds weekly concerts throughout
the year. During the winter, attend a concert at the Congregational Church, take a sleigh ride, or watch and participate
in the weekly contra dancing. Acadia National Park is about
an hour's drive north.

How to Get There.   Take I-95 to Augusta. Take Route 3
north to Belfast. Take Route 1 north to Route 15 south. Follow
Route 15 south to Blue Hill. The inn is on Union Street, in the
middle of town.

Pilgrim's Inn

Pilgrim's Inn, *Deer Isle, Maine*

Fans of the epic Civil War series on PBS will surely recognize this distinctive inn, a large maroon 1793 colonial in tiny Deer Isle Village. Vivacious innkeepers Jean and Dud Hendrick have owned this fine country inn since 1982. Not inclined to sit on their past reputation, they have recently upgraded the barn dining room and menu, added a building to the inn, and renovated rooms in the inn.

On the first floor there's a library filled with books relating to the area. On the ground level, a taproom and the wood-paneled lounge, each with a large eight-foot wood-burning fireplace, open onto the lawn that leads to the millpond. A few Adirondack chairs are set out by the water, creating a relaxing spot to sit with a good book. An old barn, now used as a gift shop, has an excellent selection of local crafts.

The guest rooms have old pumpkin pine floors and are

furnished with country antiques. Room 4, a large corner second-floor room with a white iron king-size bed, blue-and-white Laura Ashley fabric, and a newly redone bath with a marble-topped vanity, tiled shower, and small deep soaking tub, is one of the two favorite rooms. Room 5, the other favorite, has a queen-size cherry four-poster and a new bath, totally tiled, with a shower only and a sink with a marble vanity top. For the best view of the harbor stay in Room 6, a spacious front corner room with a queen-size bed with a carved Victorian high headboard, a pair of high-backed Victorian parlor chairs, and a new bath with a tiled shower and sink in the room. Room 7, with a white wicker queen-size four-poster bed and a large bath, is on the front but the view is obscured by a large tree.

The third-favorite is Room 11, on the third floor. This large room has a window seat with a view of the millpond, queen-size bed, and new bath with Deer Isle granite vanity. Other rooms on this floor are Room 14, with a queen-size bed and new bath with a granite vanity, and Rooms 9 and 10, two small rooms that share a bath.

Ginny's, a vintage house on the property with a large deck overlooking Northwest Harbor, was converted into two condo units. For privacy, longer stays, and traveling with children or pets, these are perfect. Each has a living room with a TV, kitchenette, dining area, bedroom with a queen-size bed, and bath. The two units share the large deck, and each has a small private deck.

Guests gather in the intimate bar or the two common rooms, each with an eight-foot wood-burning fireplace, at 6 each evening to chat with the innkeepers and the other guests, have a drink, and savor five to six creative hors d'oeuvres. One night we enjoyed miniature crab cakes, smoked salmon, and sliced apples served with smoked trout pâté, another night it was marinated herbed mussels, corn tortilla pizza, and a cheese fondue. The hors d'oeuvres are a signature of this inn.

At 7 P.M. dinner is served in the barn dining room, which was recently renovated with the addition of multipaned windows so diners now have a clear view of the water. A woodstove takes the chill off on cool evenings. The menu includes a choice of three appetizers, four entrées, and three desserts. Chef Terry Foster has written an excellent cookbook that includes almost all the recipes you'll find on the menu. Starters could be lobster gumbo; lobster and corn chowder; risotto with mushrooms, leeks and fontina cheese; or ravioli filled with chicken, ricotta, and Swiss chard. This is followed by a salad of greens grown in the inn's garden and homemade bread. The main courses include a beef, salmon, and vegetarian entrée as well as a nightly special. A sampling includes roast salmon in phyllo, an incredible bouillabaisse that was served on our most recent visit, citrus herb-roasted Deer Isle farm chicken, paella, and herb crusted tenderloin of beef with roasted peppers and shiitake mushrooms. And for dessert, choices could include a macadamia nut tart, homemade ice cream, sorbet, or fresh fruit.

If you are having a bottle of wine with dinner we suggest ordering the bottle and even sipping a glass with your hors d'oeuvres as all guests are served at the same time.

For early risers fresh brewed coffee is left out in the hallways. Breakfast, served from 8 to 9 A.M., includes a buffet of juices, cereals, and breads, plus a choice of entrée such as omelettes with bacon or sausage, blueberry pancakes, or waffles.

Open mid-May through mid-October. Fifteen rooms and suites, thirteen with private bath. Rooms with private bath $175, shared bath $150, Ginny's $205. $10 additional in July and August. Breakfast and dinner included. Bed-and-breakfast rates available. 15% service charge. Children over 10 welcome.

Third person $65. No smoking. Pets permitted in Ginny's. Bicycles available. Deer Isle, ME 04627; (207) 348-6615; fax (207) 348-7769; www.pilgrimsinn.com.

What to Do.   Communities to visit on the peninsula include Blue Hill, Castine, Deer Isle, and Stonington, all of which have many galleries, antiques shops, and craft stores. This is a major crafts area. On Deer Isle, the well-known Haystack Mountain School of Crafts and the Wooden Boat School are open in the summer only; call to find out visiting hours. Be sure to visit the Blue Heron Gallery in Deer Isle, a top craft gallery. In Blue Hill, visit two pottery factories, Rowantrees and Rackliffe; the Leighton Gallery is one of the top galleries in Maine.

Take a day's sail from Stonington, Castine, or Brooksville; take the mailboat to Isle au Haut and walk the trails; or hike to the top of Blue Hill Mountain. During the summer, attend the Kneisel Hall chamber music concerts. Acadia National Park is about an hour's drive.

How to Get There.   From Portland, take I-95 north to Augusta. Take Route 3 east to Belfast and continue on Route 3/Route 1 to Orland. Take Route 15 south to Deer Isle.

The Keeper's House

The Keeper's House, *Isle au Haut, Maine*

The Keeper's House is a most unusual inn located on rugged Isle au Haut, a little-known appendage of Acadia National Park in East Penobscot Bay, 8 miles from Stonington, Maine. There are no phones and no electricity at the inn, though a marine radio is available for emergencies. Bathrooms are shared, and the little Oil House has an outhouse. Access to Isle au Haut is a forty-minute trip by a mailboat, which makes a stop at the Keeper's House dock.

But before you tire of reading about the romantic lighting in a bed-and-breakfast without electricity, let us strongly caution that this is not a romantic hideaway for everyone. The remote nature of the island, and the frontier amenities of the inn itself, are not for those who covet large, luxuriously furnished rooms, extensive gourmet menus, and fine shops nearby. It is a great experience for those who find contentment in the splendor of thick forests and a pristine shoreline. If this is you, we cannot recommend the Keeper's House strongly enough. Go and enjoy!

The largest room of the four in the main house is the third-floor Garret Room, which has a double bed. This is the most expensive of the rooms, as one of the inn's two bathrooms is on the third floor. The other three rooms, all with double beds and one with a trundle bed, are on the second floor. The Keeper's Room, the original master bedroom and the second most expensive room, is popular for its view of the lighthouse and for its woodstove. The Sunrise Room also has a wood-stove. The Horizon Room looks westward and, in one of the innkeepers' opinion, has the best view of any room in the main house.

There is also a tiny guest cottage. The Oil House (we think of it as a dollhouse, as it is only about 10 feet square) is furnished with a double bed and a potbellied stove. Two chairs sit on a tiny deck overlooking the water; a short path leads to an outhouse, a pleasant shingled building on a scenic bluff. There's an outdoor sink and an outdoor solar-heated shower on the shore surrounded by a wood fence. While this is certainly the most primitive accommodation it has a definite appeal since it is the most private.

Before dinner you can hike or just lounge about, sipping wine (we suggest you bring a bottle, as the inn has no liquor license), nibbling hors d'oeuvres, and watching porpoise play as the sun casts shadows on the lighthouse.

All the guests sit together at two candlelit tables for dinner, which, on the day we visited, included homemade bread, eggplant Parmesan soup, baked salmon, bulgur pilaf, vegetables, and a garden salad with lettuces grown on the island. For dessert, we had a choice of apple charlotte or lemon teacake. Other entrées are generally seafood or chicken dishes such as lobster or scallops in a cream sauce served over homemade pasta. On Sunday nights innkeepers Jeff and Judi Burke serve a traditional lobster dinner, always a favorite event.

After dinner we left for our rooms with a candle. The warm rose light from the working lighthouse played on the white walls of the bedrooms. During the day guests take a picnic lunch and spend the day hiking the trails or riding the inn's bikes on the 14 miles of roads.

Open mid-May through October. Four rooms and a cottage, all sharing baths or outhouses, $255–$294 for two, including three meals a day and tax. Two-night minimum in July and August. Children welcome. Third person $50–$75 additional. No pets. No smoking. Box 26, Isle au Haut, ME 04645; (207) 367-2261 for off-island information and reservations.

What to Do. Thirty-two miles of well-groomed, rarely used national park trails crisscross the island. We enjoyed the 3.8-mile Duck Harbor Trail, which winds through a moss-carpeted forest. We got within fifty feet of an osprey nest, and we've heard there is also an eagle's nest on the island. The island's village has a one-room schoolhouse, a general store, and the Union Congregational Church. The Burkes have maps of the island and will suggest places to hike and poke around. There are also bicycles at the Keeper's House that guests can rent to bike on the dirt road around the island.

How to Get There. Stonington is about 480 miles from New York City and about 280 miles from Boston. From Portland, take I-95 north to Augusta. Take Route 3 east to Orland, then Route 15 south to Stonington. Access to Isle au Haut is by mailboat, which leaves from Stonington at about 4 P.M. For information about the mailboat schedule call (207) 367-5193.

A Little Dream

A Little Dream, *Camden, Maine*

We sat on the blue Victorian sofa in the pink-tiled sunroom, sipping a glass of strawberry iced tea and nibbling smoked trout pâté. Everywhere we looked, a vignette of artfully arranged Victoriana appeared: teddy bears, antique dolls, quilts, an old-fashioned wheelbarrow filled with plants, a teapot and cups on a little linen-covered table, piles of hatboxes, a violin propped on the mantel. "I'm a collector of collections," Joanne Ball told us when we asked how she and her husband, Billy Fontana, a sculptor, had amassed such an extraordinary collection. The four-foot-tall unicorn, the oversized teddy bears, and our favorite, a nineteenth-century Italian marionette, are part of the couple's international collection of folk art toys attractively displayed throughout the inn.

The living room has a gas fireplace, chintz-covered easy chairs and sofas, ribboned baskets stacked with magazines, a bottle of sherry on a silver tray, and long-stemmed glasses

filled with candy. "During the winter the house has a particularly romantic feel," Joanne said. "Then we can really pamper
our guests and breakfast can be served as late as the guests
wish."

The Master Bedroom has a king-size canopy bed facing a
television and VCR, a chaise longue, and a private deck with
a table and chairs. The Blue Turret Room, a first-floor room
that faces Route 1, has a gas fireplace, queen-size bed, English
walnut mirror-front armoire, and white wicker rockers placed
in the bay window. The adjacent Peach Room has a queen-
size bed and is available if there's a third person in the group.
Travels is a second-floor room with a queen-size bed, small
private deck, and bath with a large shower (no tub). The Toy
Room, a little museum or a sitting room, houses many of
Joanne and Billy's toys, including the tall unicorn rocking
horse at the bay window.

They have recently finished the construction of an addition
to the Carriage House building. The lowest level is Billy's
studio. Directly above this is a new studio, the largest room,
with a king-size bed, gas fireplace, sitting area with a bay window, and a large private porch area. Treetops, the front Carriage House unit on the third level, is a bright and airy suite.
It has a tiny bedroom with a queen-size brass bed, a spacious
living room with a wet bar, and a large deck with a far view
of Curtis Island. The back Carriage House unit has a cozy,
private feel with a queen-size bed, a wet bar, a steep spiral
staircase leading to a low-ceilinged loft sitting room, and a tiny
balcony overlooking the back garden.

At night a breakfast menu is put outside your door so
that you can indicate the time you want breakfast, which variety of gourmet coffee or tea you prefer, and whether you'd
like a smoked salmon, Brie-and-apple, or cheddar-cheese-
and-ham omelette. The candlelit table in the dining room is a
scene of elaborate Victorian perfection: lacy cloths, stemmed

glassware, and a decorative cake plate with the day's sweet bread under a glass dome. The breakfast entrée changes daily but might include fruit crepes, heart-shaped banana-pecan waffles, smoked trout with vichyssoise sauce and dilled eggs, or lemon ricotta soufflé pancakes served with raspberry sauce.

Six rooms and suites, each with private bath. Memorial Day through October, $110–$195; other times of the year, $95–$140. Afternoon tea and full breakfast included. Not appropriate for children. No pets. No smoking. Two-night minimum weekends, holidays, and month of August. 66 High Street (Route 1), Camden, ME 04843; (207) 236-8742; fax (207) 236-8742.

Where to Dine. In season, Miller's Lobster in Spruce Head is the quintessential lobster-in-the-rough spot. It's located at the end of a dirt road in a quiet cove (off Route 73 between South Thomaston and St. George; (207) 594-7406).

The fashionable Belmont (6 Belmont Avenue, Camden; (207) 236-8053) is the place to go for fine dining. For a more casual atmosphere and large portions we like Frog Water Café (Elm Street, Camden; (207) 236-8998). The Sea Dog brew pub, located in a restored old mill in the center of town (43 Mechanic Street, Camden; (207) 236-6863), has a spectacular setting with a wall of glass overlooking the river. On Main Street, in the center of town, is Cappy's Restaurant and sailors' bar, a local hangout (207) 236-2254).

What to Do. During the summer you can hike in Camden Hills State Park or take a day or overnight windjammer cruise. Go out on the *Lively Lady* to learn how to catch lobsters, or rent a kayak for a two-hour harbor tour. Camden has a number of good shops and galleries. The views at Camden and Rockport Harbors or at Owls Head Lighthouse are so spectacular that you could easily spend the afternoon just watching the boats come and go.

The Farnsworth Art Museum, in nearby Rockland, has an emphasis on New England artists. We went there because of our particular interest in seeing the Wyeth paintings of local Maine scenes. Visit the nearby Owls Head Transportation Museum to see vintage cars and airplanes, especially on certain weekends, when they "come alive." Head north to the Maritime Museum and antiques jaunts in Searsport. Head south to the Pemaquid Point Lighthouse, one of the most photographed on the coast. Monhegan Island is a great place to walk the trails and visit artists' studios.

How to Get There.   Take 1-95 north to the Route 1 exit just before Brunswick. Follow Route 1 north to Camden. The inn is located on the left side of the road just north of the center of Camden.

Squire Tarbox Inn

Squire Tarbox Inn, *Wiscasset, Maine*

"**W**e want to be known as a country inn at the end of a road to nowhere," Bill and Karen Mitman told us as we sat by one of the inn's wood-burning fireplaces, sampling goat cheese that they make from the milk of their Nubian goats. The inn is located south of Wiscasset on Westport Island, which so far has escaped the attention of developers. That's to the liking of Bill and Karen, whose strong interest in country life led them to this quiet location twelve years ago. In addition to the goats, who are the star attractions at the inn, the Mitmans also have a horse, two donkeys, and several chickens.

The inn is a collection of connecting Maine buildings from different centuries. The original 1763 cape house was moved to this location in the 1820s. Original owner Samuel Tarbox added a Federal-style home, which the Mitmans have restored. Each of the four large rooms in this building has a wood-burning fireplace. Two have king-size beds, one has a queen-size bed and the fourth room has a double and a single bed. The other seven rooms are the barn rooms, four of which open off the casual double-story barn sitting room; the other three have private entrances. We chose Room 5, a small, low-ceilinged room in the barn, for the balcony and view of the bird feeders outside our Dutch door. We spied a pair of Baltimore orioles, hummingbirds, and evening grosbeaks. All of the rooms have electric mattresses, great for chilly Maine nights.

The woodstove in the barn's common room was lit early in the morning, making the room a cozy place to peruse a carefully selected collection of books. The front living room features a wood-burning fireplace and a bowl of chocolate chip cookies. Help yourself to a drink at the honor bar, then head out to the newly reconstructed 1820 post-and-beam barn with two rope swings, or beyond to the goats' sheds, which are kept extremely clean. A 1,000-foot path leads through a wooded area to a saltwater inlet where there is a floating dock, a rowboat for guests' use, and a small screened building with two chairs. Stay a few days and you'll soon adjust to the easy rhythm of this idyllic spot.

Dining at this unique farm/inn is a memorable experience, far more than just a delicious dinner by a wood-burning fireplace. It begins with an informal cocktail hour at 6 P.M. that features a sampling of goat cheese made at the inn's small licensed cheese plant. We tried a creamy chèvre with chives and garlic, a tellicherry crottin rolled in cracked pepper, and an aged Caerphilly that had a smooth texture and a mellow flavor. Some of the guests gathered around an old-fashioned player piano, some relaxed by the fireplace or the woodstoves in rooms filled with interesting books about Maine, and others strolled down to the water.

The walls in the dining room are old barn boards, and a

brick fireplace creates the ambience. We were seated with two other couples who were staying at the inn. A single-entrée four-course dinner is served each evening, although substitutions can be arranged. We started with mushrooms stuffed with spinach and walnuts, followed by a salad of mixed greens with balsamic vinaigrette dressing. Slightly sweet buns made from goat whey are a welcome staple on the menu. Our entrée, boneless breast of chicken stuffed with herbed chèvre encased in a puff pastry shell, was accompanied by fresh asparagus, honey-glazed baby carrots, and pan-roasted potatoes. Dessert was an orange-almond tart with whipped cream. Other nights, the main entrée might be grilled swordfish, roast pork, broiled scallops, or poached salmon.

After dessert, diners are invited to the shed to watch the goats being milked. Chief goat-milker and cheese-maker Karen Mitman explains the process. On a recent visit, a baby goat not more than twenty-four hours old seemed to enjoy being the center of attention. The breakfast buffet includes fruit, home-baked breads, goat cheese, and granola.

Open mid-May through October. Eleven rooms, each with private bath; four rooms with fireplaces, $85–$175, breakfast included; $143–$245, breakfast and dinner included. 12% service charge. No pets. Dinner served nightly to outside guests by advance reservation only. Cocktails, 6 P.M.; dinner, 7 P.M. Prix fixe, $33. RR 2, Box 620, Wiscasset, ME 04578; (207) 882-7693; fax (207) 882-7107; www.squiretarboxinn.com.

What to Do.   This rugged rock-strewn shoreline and the people who call this area of Maine home have been fertile territory for artists for the past 150 years. You can see their paintings in the Portland Museum of Art and the Walker Art Building at Bowdoin College. At the Maine Maritime Museum in Bath you can see and experience 400 years of Maine's seagoing history. Drive down to Reid State Park, an idyllic spot for a picnic at tables on the rocky coast, to watch and listen to the rhythms of the sea. Or stop at the Osprey in Robinhood for lunch (at the marina off Route 127).

Wiscasset is one of the prettiest villages in Maine, with many houses once owned by sea captains. Take a tour of the Musical Wonder House in Wiscasset to see and hear an incredible collection of music boxes. Wiscasset also has a variety of antiques shops, most of which are on Main Street. Drive down and around the many fingers of land that protrude into the ocean. Visit Boothbay Harbor and continue to East Boothbay and Ocean Point, one of the great panoramas of the Maine coastline.

How to Get There.   Take I-95 north to the Route 1 exit just before Brunswick. Follow Route 1 through Bath. Take Route 144 (before you get to Wiscasset) south for 8.5 miles. The inn is located on Route 144 on Westport Island.

Inn by the Sea

Inn by the Sea, *Cape Elizabeth, Maine*

This recently built gray-shingled complex located twenty minutes south of Portland bordering Crescent Beach State Park includes a main building and four cottage buildings. It is distinguished from other types of accommodations in the area because all of the rooms are large suites with full kitchens. Guests have the option of cooking their own meals, dining in the restaurant, or ordering room service. The accommodations are so spacious that a few of the units are rented on a long-term basis.

The lobby is marble-tiled, its walls decorated with original elephant folio Audubon prints of seacoast birds. There is an outdoor pool, a tennis court, and a boardwalk that leads to a long sandy beach and a harbor that is used by lobstermen. The inn provides bicycles and beach chairs.

There are twenty-five suites in the main building that have

plush carpeting and contemporary-styled furnishings. We particularly like the two-level Loft Suites. On the lower level there is a full kitchen, a spacious living room with a wall of windows, a two-story cathedral ceiling, and a small deck that overlooks the swimming pool. Half of the second floor is a loft bedroom and an oversized bath with a deep soaking tub big enough for two as well as a separate shower. Amenities include televisions in the bedroom and the living room, three phones, a basket with more than the usual toiletries, and turndown service if requested. The Garden Suites are the other type of room in the main building. These one-level suites are furnished similarly to the Loft Suites but are not quite as spacious. These each have an entrance off an interior hallway as well as an outdoor patio entrance that leads to the pool area.

There are eighteen cottage units located in four buildings. These are particularly nice for a summer stay since they are decorated with wicker and pine furnishings and have an airy feel with wide wraparound porches or decks and expansive views of the marsh grasses and the ocean in the distance. All of the cottage units have two bedrooms; some are on two levels with skylights and peaked ceilings and others are on one level.

The best cottage units are in the Beach House. These are each two floors with a woodstove in the living room and a larger deck area. The Mahaney Suite is the very best unit in the Beach House as it is the largest and has a full front water view. None of the suites in the main inn or the cottages are air-conditioned, generally never a problem as the inn is on the ocean. Dogs are permitted and even catered to; innkeepers provide dog bowls and leave a dog bone for pet turndown service.

Should you want to cook your own lobster (also available precooked) the inn will procure lobsters from a local lobsterman. The inn will even do your grocery shopping, a delightful plus.

You might want to bring your own food and have breakfast in your suite or out on your deck; the inn serves breakfast in the dining room daily. On one of the days of your stay we suggest you splurge on eggs Benedict—or better yet, on the inn's special variation made with fresh lobster meat.

The restaurant, an attractive airy-feeling dining room, has a view of the water. For summer dining we like the porch room, particularly the tables with a water view.

There are always a couple of lobster preparations on the menu. Duck breast on a salad of spinach and arugula, spinach greens, and caramelized walnuts with grilled portabello mushrooms and warm bacon dressing; lobster bisque; or lobster ravioli are starters. Mixed seafood grill, crab cakes, grilled marinated chicken, grilled Thai sea scallops, shrimp Szechuan, rack of lamb, grilled tournedos, and a combination of lobster, shrimp, and scallops served over angel-hair pasta with peppers and asparagus are some of the entrées.

Forty-three one-and two-bedroom suites, all with full kitchens. July and August, $180–$410; other times of the year, $125–$280. Packages available midweek and off-season. Breakfast, lunch, and dinner daily. Lunch entrées $7–$11. Dinner entrées $10–$25. Children welcome. Pets permitted. Route 77, Cape Elizabeth, ME 04107; (207) 799-3134, (800) 888-IBTS; fax (207) 799-4779; www.innbythesea.com.

What to Do. Facilities at the inn include an outdoor swimming pool, a tennis court, and bicycles. A boardwalk leads from the inn to Crescent Beach State Park, a grand sand beach overlooking the Atlantic Ocean. For a pleasant excursion bicycle north on Route 77 to the Shore Road to the Portland Head Light, the most photographed lighthouse in Maine. On your return, take Two Lights Road and have lunch at Two

Lights Lobster Shack. Bicycle south on Route 77 to Prouts Neck to see beautiful homes with great water views and to visit Winslow Homer's studio. In Portland, called little San Francisco by the many professionals and artists who have moved here in the past decade, visit the Portland Museum of Art, noted for its collection of French Impressionists and its large collection of Winslow Homer's paintings, and the Old Port Exchange area, where there are good galleries, craft shops, and excellent restaurants. Our favorites are Fore Street, 288 Fore Street, an informal restaurant with open kitchen, brick oven, rotisserie, and water views; Street and Co., located on a narrow cobblestone street in the Old Port; and Back Bay Grill. Take the mail and freight boat that visits six of the 135 islands in Casco Bay. And there is Freeport (about a half-hour's drive), home to legendary L. L. Bean and 100 outlets, where you can "shop till you drop"—a good option, particularly for a rainy day.

How to Get There.   Take the Maine Turnpike (I-95) to exit 7. Follow to the junction of Route 1. Turn right on Route 1; turn left on Pleasant Hill Road to Route 77. Turn left on Route 77, follow to Inn by the Sea, on the right.

The Inn at Harbor Head

Inn at Harbor Head, *Kennebunkport, Maine*

This waterfront deluxe artistically-decorated inn overlooks the harbor of Cape Porpoise, 2.5 miles from the center of Kennebunkport. The new owners are Dick and Eve Roesler, who purchased the inn in March 1998.

The Summer Suite is a favorite room, with a striking water view, a balcony with a wrought iron love seat, and a fireplace. The large bathroom has a double whirlpool tub, a peaked ceiling, a skylight, and a bidet. The king-size bed is covered with a black flowered chintz bedspread. White wicker furniture and a white wicker chaise longue set for viewing the water add to the summer breezy feeling.

The newly renovated three-room Harbor Suite is now the top room in the inn. It is a good choice during the spring, fall, and winter as it has a fireplace. It is equally nice for a summer stay as it has a private deck with rocking chairs. The bedroom has a king-size canopy bed with a view of the water as well as the fireplace in the sitting room. The bath chamber is luxurious with a clawfoot soaking tub facing French doors that open onto a balcony as well as a separate small bath with a shower. A trompe l'oeil mural with scenes of the fishing harbor cover the walls of one room and another mural of the harbor islands decorates the other room.

You'll notice a Japanese influence in the small Garden Room, especially the river pebbles next to the walls at the entrance. The room has a stately four-poster queen-size bed with a tapestry duvet and the same glorious view as the Summer Suite. French doors open onto a private deck, set with a table and chairs, that offers a beautiful view of the water.

The Ocean Room, the smallest in the inn, has a massive queen-size plantation bed with hidden jewelry spaces in the foot posts and an antique pine armoire and bureau. A collection of books about ocean voyages and shipwreck tales fills the shelves of this room.

This is an inn where one is happy to stay put, lounging in the hammocks, sketching by the water, watching the loons and the seals, and listening to the foghorns and seagulls. When the weather is cool guests sit in the library, which has a grand gas log fireplace, Oriental rugs, a couch, and comfortable chairs set by the picture windows with marvelous views of the harbor and the ocean. From 4 to 5:30 they serve a high tea in the formal living room that includes tea sandwiches and dessert.

Elegant breakfasts, served at 8:30 A.M. with guests sitting at one table, always include freshly squeezed orange juice, a fruit course, an entrée, and freshly baked breads. The fruit course might be broiled bananas, pears served with peach coulis, or peaches and blueberries in spiced white wine. Typical entrées include pecan French toast, tropical waffles with macadamia nuts and toasted coconut, and eggs Florentine.

Four rooms, each with private bath. Late May to late

October and Christmas Prelude weekends, $190–$295; other times, $145–$195. Full breakfast and afternoon hors d'oeuvres included. Children over 12 welcome. Third person in the Harbor Suite $25 additional. No pets. No smoking. Two-night weekend minimum. 41 Pier Road, Kennebunkport, ME 04046-6916; (207) 967-5564; fax (207) 967-1294; www.harborhead.com.

Where to Dine.   For romantic, elegant dining we suggest the White Barn Inn (37 Beach Street, Kennebunkport; (207) 967-2321). We feel that its food and service are the best in the area. The main room is a two-story restored barn. Salt Marsh Tavern is another top choice for a romantic candlelit dinner. For informal dining we like Grissini (27 Western Avenue, Kennebunk; (207) 967-2211), which specializes in Tuscan fare such as creative pizzas cooked in a wood-fired adobe pizza oven and homemade pastas.

If you don't want to leave the seclusion of Cape Porpoise, walk down the street to Seascapes (Cape Porpoise Harbor, Cape Porpoise; (207) 967-8500), which specializes in creative seafood dishes and has a dining room overlooking the working harbor of Cape Porpoise. For lobster-in-the-rough during the summer, visit the traditional Nunan's Lobster Hut (Route 9, Cape Porpoise; (207) 967-4435), a run-down, much-beloved institution with picnic tables, lobsters, steamers, and blueberry pie. Also in Cape Porpoise is the Cape Pier Chowder House, a shack perched on the edge of the water, which is a good lunch stop for fried clams or lobster. You can get lobster year-round at the Lobster Pot restaurant (Route 9, Cape Porpoise; (207) 967-4268).

What to Do.   Spend a day in Kennebunkport visiting the galleries. Stroll along Parson's Way, a stretch of paths overlooking the Atlantic Ocean with benches at intervals. Walker's

Point, former president George Bush's summer home, is along this road.

The beaches are some of the finest in Maine. They are clean and not crowded. This is Maine, however; the water is cold. Beaches in the area that we like include Kennebunk Beach, Goose Rocks Beach, and Parson's Beach. The Rachel Carson Wildlife Refuge is a pleasant place to take a walk and learn about the salt marsh ecosystem. Drive to Ogunquit, about 15 miles south of Kennebunkport, to see a play at the Ogunquit summer theater and walk the Marginal Way, a mile-long footpath along the cliffs overlooking uninterrupted vistas of the Atlantic Ocean. The discount stores in Freeport are a good option for a rainy day, and L. L. Bean, of course, is a Maine institution.

How to Get There. Take I-95 north to exit 3, then take Route 35 east, following signs to Kennebunkport. Route 9 intersects with Route 35 at Kennebunkport. Follow Route 9 east about 2 miles from Kennebunkport to Cape Porpoise. Leave Route 9 where it turns sharp left; go straight ahead .25 mile past the Wayfarer Restaurant to the inn, on your right.

© David Allen

The main dining room at The White Barn Inn

White Barn Inn, *Kennebunkport, Maine*

This hideaway, a deluxe country house hotel .25 mile from the ocean on a quiet street in Kennebunkport, combines truly spectacular formal dining in a dramatic setting with spacious, well-appointed rooms. The owner/innkeeper is Laurie Bongiorno.

The top accommodations are the large one-room suites with two-person whirlpool tubs and fireplaces. (The fireplaces in the main building are gas and the ones in the other buildings are wood-burning.) All the rooms have phones, air-conditioning, televisions, and CD players (on request if you stay in the inn). The suites have VCRs, and there's a selection of tapes to borrow.

May's Annex is a carriage house with six spacious deluxe rooms, each about 23 feet long. The rooms have a sitting area at one end with a wood-burning fireplace with couches or large easy chairs and a coffee table set in front of it, a king-size four-poster bed, plush wall-to-wall carpeting, a phone, and an armoire that hides the television. The large bathrooms have marble floors, single-size whirlpool baths, a separate glass-enclosed, marble-lined shower with a pulsating shower head, and thick terry cloth robes. All the rooms in this building are practically identical except for the Red Suite, our favorite, as it is the only room with a deck and chairs.

May's Cottage was reconfigured and is now a single room with a king-size bed and a double-sided wood-burning fireplace that you can see from the bed and from the living room. The bath has a double whirlpool tub and separate shower. And there's a small deck that overlooks the pool.

The four Poolhouse Rooms, smaller than those in the Annex, are in a third outbuilding. Each has a queen-size sleigh bed, a wood-burning fireplace, and a bath with a single whirlpool tub, granite sink, and floors.

Most of the rooms in the main inn, the original farmhouse, are modest in size but are plushly appointed. The rooms in this building have a New England feel with print wallpaper, hand-painted furniture, and double, queen, or twin beds. Two new suites are located in the main inn. One, as large as the rooms in May's Annex, has a double whirlpool tub and a three-sided gas fireplace. The second is above the restaurant and includes an even larger gas fireplace, a two-person whirlpool tub, and the only private deck in the main inn.

All of the rooms are provided with fresh fruit, mineral water, flowers, and a personalized newsletter at turndown. Other facilities include a new attractively landscaped pool with a waterfall edge and complimentary use of the inn's bicycles. Tea is available between 3 and 4 P.M. in one of the small parlors off the foyer.

Breakfast includes freshly squeezed orange juice, a basket of pastries, a fruit plate, and an assortment of cereals. A full breakfast is available for an additional fee.

The candlelit main dining room is a classic New England barn with seasoned wood interior walls with oil paintings, exposed rafters, and a second floor filled with an assortment of artfully arranged items one might have found stashed in an old barn: a hay rake, old steamer trunks, baskets, pulleys, a pair of ice tongs, a rocking chair, scales, and old signs advertising elixirs, old harnesses, and house paints. A large picture window in each of the two barn dining rooms looks onto a viewing porch seasonally decorated with bales of hay or corn stalks, old rocking chairs, a wooden sleigh, farm tools, and pots of flowers. At the front of the main dining room, our preference of the two barn dining rooms, there are cocktail tables and a piano bar. A new wine cellar dining room has seating for up to sixteen.

The exceptionally knowledgeable staff serves in a formal elegant manner; each dish is brought from the kitchen by a waiter and all are served simultaneously. Without a doubt this is the best dining in the area.

The menu changes weekly and includes a choice of about eight appetizers, eight entrées, and six desserts. Dinner includes a selection of hors d'oeuvres, an appetizer, sorbet or soup as a palate cleanser, entrée, and dessert. For starters we were particularly impressed with the lobster spring roll and the cappuccino mushroom soup of shiitake and oyster mushrooms with foie gras. Steamed tender lobster on a bed of homemade fettuccine was a memorable entrée that we highly recommend. Other choices are a combination dish of roasted

rack of lamb encrusted with pecans and roasted leg of venison, breast of farm-raised chicken with portabello mushrooms
wrapped in pastry, and grilled Maine salmon on a bed of vegetables. For dessert we suggest the caramelized apples with
calvados ice cream, caramel sauce, and a phyllo flower; and
the trio of chocolate desserts, including a terrine, a mousse,
and a sorbet.

Twenty-five rooms and suites, each with private bath. June
through October, $160–$350; other times, $130–$320. Breakfast and tea included. Two-night weekend minimum. Children
over 12 welcome. Rooms are double occupancy only. No
smoking in the rooms. No pets. Dinner daily April through
December, Wednesday through Sunday mid-January through
March. Jackets required. Prix fixe $62.37 Beach Street, Box
560C, Kennebunkport, ME 04046; (207) 967-2321; fax (207)
967-1100; www.whitebarninn.com.

Where to Dine.   Although the White Barn Inn itself is by
far the best place to dine in Kennebunkport, we also suggest
Grissini (27 Western Avenue, Kennebunk; (207) 967-2211), a
Tuscan-style restaurant also owned by Laurie Bongiorno of
the White Barn Inn. The atmosphere is sophisticated yet comfortable: parchment paper covers the tables, the ceiling has
exposed pipes, and there's a stone patio for outdoor dining.
Slices of different kinds of homemade bread are placed directly on the table; tear off pieces and dip them into the olive
oil. Have a large or a small dinner. Tuscan white bean soup
with duck sausage or pizza topped with combinations such as
scallops, mussels, and calamari or goat cheese and pesto combined with a salad make a great meal. Homemade pasta combinations include pappardelle with shiitake, oyster, and
portabello mushrooms; linguini with seafood; fetttuccine with
grilled chicken, pesto, and brandied apples; and tagliolini with
pesto and pine nuts. There's also wood-grilled chicken with

Tuscan mashed potatoes, osso buco, and Maine trout steamed in foil. Tiramisu and strawberries with balsamic vinegar and mascarpone cheese are some of the desserts.

What to Do.   From the inn it is only a .25-mile walk to Kennebunk Beach, but for more seclusion we suggest Parson's Beach and Goose Rocks Beach. In Kennebunkport, visit galleries and shops and stroll along Parson's Way, a path that overlooks the Atlantic Ocean, to Walker's Point, former president George Bush's summer home. Shopping enthusiasts will want to spend time at the discount shops in Freeport.

How to Get There.   Take the Maine Turnpike (I-95) north to exit 3. Follow Route 35 south for 6 miles toward Kennebunkport. At the intersection of Routes 35 and 9 continue straight on Beach Street (Route 35) for .25 mile to the inn.

The Captain Lord Mansion

The Captain Lord Mansion,
Kennebunkport, Maine

"**W**e sell romance," declared Bev Davis, who, along with husband Rick Litchfield, owns and operates this distinguished mansion built in 1812 by a sea captain and situated in Kennebunkport on a hill at the edge of the town green. The moment you step into the high-ceilinged, antiques-filled, Oriental-carpeted common room, you will sense a quiet elegance. The furnishings in the bedrooms are nineteenth-century antiques with gas fireplaces. To provide comfort for today's travelers, the massive, high four-poster beds have all been "stretched" to accommodate king-size and queen-size mattresses. All the rooms, named after ships that sailed in Captain Lord's fleet, are air-conditioned and have phones, and fourteen have gas fireplaces. The deluxe rooms have small, well-stocked minibars that operate on the honor system;

guests in the other rooms help themselves to juices and sodas from the inn's refrigerator, also on the honor system.

First-and second-floor rooms have nine-and-a-half-foot ceilings. The top accommodations are the six rooms on the front of the inn, with a view of the river. The new Captain's Suite (which includes the room formerly called Brig Merchant), on the first floor, is the most deluxe. The bedroom of the suite has a king-size canopy bed and a fireplace, Schumacher wallpaper, an English dressing table, and a massive armoire with a writing desk in the center. The toilet room has a marble floor and a hydro-massage shower. The next room is lined with mirrors and includes a double-whirlpool tub, a fireplace, double pedestal sinks, exercise equipment, and a television. The Oriental Room, also on the first floor, has a queen-size canopy bed, a fireplace, and a park view.

The river-view rooms on the second floor are the Lincoln Room, with an 1820 English four-poster queen-size bed, a marble bath with a heated floor, and a large marble shower; and Excelsior, with a king-size bed. Both rooms have fireplaces. Champion is a suite with a queen-size canopy bed, a sitting room with a fireplace, and a bath with an antique soaking tub and shower.

Third-floor Ship Harvest, a river-view room, has a country look with a king-size four-poster bed, a mural scene of Kennebunkport in the 1800s, country decorations including an old cobbler's bench and a roulette wheel from a Maine country fair, and a bath with a heated floor and a double sink. Regulator, another river-view room, also has a king-size bed. Union is a deluxe room with a king-size bed and a bath with a heated floor and a double whirlpool tub.

Breakfast is served family style at two long tables in the country kitchen with two seatings daily. It includes muffins, breads, and fruit followed by a hot entrée such as vegetable quiche, Belgian waffles, or malted blueberry pancakes.

For a family or a few people traveling together we particularly like Phoebe's Fantasy, a separate building with four rooms, two with king-size beds and two with queen-size beds. The common gathering room has a large-screen television, a fireplace, and an attractive plush chintz sofa. Guests who stay at Phoebe's Fantasy are served their breakfast in this building, and because there is a maximum of eight people in this building, there is only one seating, allowing you to linger as long as you wish.

Twenty rooms and suites, each with private bath. June through December, $175–$375; other times, $99–$299. Afternoon tea and full breakfast included. Children over 6 welcome. Third person $10–$25. No pets. No smoking. Two-night weekend minimum. Box 800, Kennebunkport, ME 04046; (207) 967-3141; fax (207) 967-3172; www.captainlord.com.

Where to Dine.   For romantic, elegant dining we suggest the White Barn Inn (37 Beach Street, Kennebunkport; (207) 967-2321). We feel that its food and service are the best in the area. The main room is a two-story restored barn. Seascapes (Cape Porpoise Harbor; (207) 967-8500) specializes in creative seafood dishes and has a dining room overlooking the working harbor of Cape Porpoise. For informal dining we like Grissini (27 Western Avenue, Kennebunk; (207) 967-2211), which specializes in Tuscan fare such as creative pizzas cooked in a wood-fired adobe pizza oven and homemade pastas. For lobster-in-the-rough go to Nunan's Lobster Hut in Cape Porpoise (May to mid-October; Route 9, Cape Porpoise; (207) 967-4435).

What to Do.   Spend a day in Kennebunkport visiting the galleries. Stroll along Parson's Way, a stretch of paths overlooking the Atlantic Ocean, with benches at intervals. Walker's Point, former president George Bush's summer home, is along this road.

The beaches are some of the finest in Maine. They are clean and not crowded. This is Maine, however; the water is cold. Beaches in the area that we like include: Kennebunk Beach, Goose Rocks Beach, and Parson's Beach. The Rachel Carson Wildlife Refuge is a pleasant place to take a walk and learn about the salt marsh ecosystem. Drive to Ogunquit, about 15 miles south of Kennebunkport, to see a play at the Ogunquit summer theater and walk the Marginal Way, a mile-long footpath along the cliffs overlooking uninterrupted vistas of the Atlantic Ocean. The discount stores in Freeport are a good option for a rainy day, and L. L. Bean, of course, is a Maine institution.

How to Get There.   Take the Maine Turnpike (I-95) north to exit 3 (Kennebunk). Turn left onto Route 35 south. At the intersection of Routes 1 and 35 continue on Route 35 to Kennebunk. Take Route 9 across the bridge over Kennebunk River and turn right onto Ocean Avenue. The inn is a few blocks down the street on your left.

Bufflehead Cove Inn

Bufflehead Cove Inn, *Kennebunkport, Maine*

Named for the diving sea ducks that winter here, Bufflehead Cove Inn is located on six private acres at the end of a gravel lane that winds past several small ponds less than a mile from the center of Kennebunkport. The location on the banks of the Kennebunk River is so peaceful that we could happily stay on the porch or the viewing deck by the water for hours, reading and looking at the myriad of waterfowl. Innkeepers Harriet and Jim Gott are natives of the area. Jim is also a lobsterman.

The living room and dining area encompass most of the first floor. The ceiling has exposed wooden beams. One side of this comfortable informal room has a wood-burning fireplace, sofa, and easy chairs. Hot water and a selection of teas, coffee, or hot chocolate are left out for the guests to help themselves.

For total privacy we suggest the Hideaway, a large airy deluxe room with a private porch and floor-to-ceiling windows that overlook the cove. The Hideaway is attached to the house but has its own private entrance and a porch that overlooks the cove. A double-sided gas fireplace separates the king-size bed from the sitting area. The room has a Bose wave radio, lots of books, and a separate bath with a skylight over the double whirlpool tub.

The Balcony Room is a new deluxe spacious room with a king-size bed, a gas fireplace, a window seat with a water view, and a sitting area by the fireplace. The balcony overlooks the river and has removable windows so you can comfortably sit there at all times of the year. In one corner there's a double-size whirlpool tub on a raised platform from which you can see the fireplace. By request, Harriet will serve breakfast in their rooms to guests staying in the Hideaway or the Balcony Rooms.

The Cove Suite is two rooms with a gas fireplace in the living room and a balcony overlooking the cove. The River Room is a smaller room with a balcony and a queen-size bed. The Garden Studio, the only room with no water view, is a spacious accommodation with its own entrance. It includes a bedroom with a queen-size bed, a bath with a skylight and a glass-enclosed shower, a large sitting area, lots of books, and a private courtyard overlooking the gardens. This is the one room where pets are permitted. All the rooms have terry cloth robes, decanters of sherry, and turndown service, which includes chocolate truffles.

Wine and cheese are set out at 5:30 P.M. Breakfast is served from 8:30 to 9:30 A.M.—outside in the summer at five tables, or inside with guests sitting at two tables. On our most recent visit we had fresh squeezed orange juice, blueberries, sweet bread, and an entrée of French toast stuffed with cream cheese and garnished with apples and bacon.

Five rooms and suites, each with private bath. June through October, $135–$250; other times, $95–$175. Full breakfast and afternoon wine and cheese included. Children over 12 welcome. Pets with permission. No smoking. Two-night minimum. Box 499, Kennebunkport, ME 04046; 207-967-3879; fax (207) 967-3879; www.dbanet.com/bcove.

Where to Dine.   For romantic, elegant dining we suggest the White Barn Inn (37 Beach Street, Kennebunkport; (207) 967-2321). We feel that its food and service are the best in the area. The main room is a two-story restored barn. Seascapes (Cape Porpoise Harbor; (207) 967-8500) specializes in creative seafood dishes and has a dining room overlooking the working harbor of Cape Porpoise. For informal dining we like Grissini (27 Western Avenue, Kennebunk; (207) 967-2211), which specializes in Tuscan fare such as creative pizzas cooked in a wood-fired adobe pizza oven and homemade pastas. For lobster-in-the-rough go to Nunan's Lobster Hut in Cape Porpoise (May to mid-October; Route 9, Cape Porpoise; (207) 967-4435).

What to Do.   Spend a day in Kennebunkport visiting the galleries. Stroll along Parson's Way, a stretch of paths overlooking the Atlantic Ocean, with benches at intervals. Walker's Point, former president George Bush's summer home, is along this road.

The beaches are some of the finest in Maine. They are clean and not crowded. This is Maine, however; the water is cold. Beaches in the area that we like include: Kennebunk Beach, Goose Rocks Beach, and Parson's Beach. The Rachel Carson Wildlife Refuge is a pleasant place to take a walk and learn about the salt marsh ecosystem. Drive to Ogunquit, about 15 miles south of Kennebunkport, to see a play at the Ogunquit summer theater and walk the Marginal Way, a mile-long footpath along the cliffs overlooking uninterrupted vistas of the Atlantic Ocean. The discount stores in Freeport are a good option for a rainy day, and L. L. Bean, of course, is a Maine institution.

How to Get There.   Take the Maine Turnpike (I-95) north to exit 3 (Kennebunk). Turn left onto Route 35 south. At the intersection of Routes 1 and 35 continue on Route 35 for 3.1 miles. Watch on the left for the inn's sign. Turn left and follow the gravel lane to the inn.

Adair

Adair, *Bethlehem, New Hampshire*

This large white three-story mansion sits on 200 acres at the northern edge of the White Mountains of New Hampshire. The Connecticut River Valley Georgian Colonial Revival home was built in 1927 by a noted Washington trial lawyer as a wedding gift for his daughter. In 1992 it was converted from a private home to a comfortable inn. The innkeepers are Bill and Judy Whitman. The large front center entry hall opens into a large living room with a wood-burning fireplace and groupings of sofas and easy chairs. To the left of the main hall is the dining room. The basement Granite Tap Room is another huge room with an honor bar, a stocked refrigerator with complimentary sodas and juices, a television with a VCR and a collection of movies, a piano, games, and a 1927 pool table. There is also a huge granite fireplace in this room. The wooded property includes a water garden with goldfish, and a tennis court.

At the top of the wide staircase take note of the attractively displayed hat collection that was found in one of the attics. Guests often get a kick out of trying on the hats. This floor has four good-sized rooms, three of which have gas fireplaces. Lafayette, the suite, is the largest with a tall queen-size four-poster bed and French doors opening to a sitting room with a fireplace stove and a fainting couch. Waterford has a queen-size bed with a massive mahogany headboard and a fireplace, and Cabot also has a queen-size four-poster bed with a fireplace. Lincoln is a smaller room with a Scottish four-poster bed and an armoire.

The four rooms on the third floor have wall-to-wall rose-colored carpeting. Three have king/twin-size beds with color-coordinated padded headboards, and one has a queen-size bed. If you need to have a phone in your room ask for the king-bedded Concord or Dalton Rooms, which have phone jacks.

The most deluxe and newest accommodation is Kinsman, with a king-size sleigh bed and a Vermont Castings gas fireplace, a deck, and a bath with an oversize double whirlpool tub and a separate shower.

Tea, along with sweet breads or cookies is served at 4 P.M. A cheese platter and beverages are set out in the game room before dinner. Bill and Judy do the breakfast, which is served between 8:30 and 9:30 A.M. and always features steaming hot popovers, their house specialty. It also includes juice, granola, hot and cold cereals, plus a hot entrée. We were served baked egg blossoms, a mixture of cheese and eggs in a flaky phyllo crust. Other favorites are eggs Benedict, and French toast made with cinnamon raisin bread and Bailey's Irish Cream.

At night the dining room is transformed into Tim-Bir Alley Restaurant. Oriental-patterned-fabric-covered walls, a gas fireplace, candles, and Queen Anne–style chairs create an upscale, relaxed atmosphere.

Tim and Biruta Carr, who formerly owned Tim-Bir Alley in Littleton, run the restaurant at the inn. The menu changes weekly. We started with the roasted eggplant garlic soup and the curried sweet potato ravioli with toasted pecan sauce. Entrées included catfish with an herb crust and roasted red pepper purée, and breast of chicken with braised cabbage and basil-beet-infused olive oil. They always garnish the plates with a selection of five or six small portions of imaginative vegetable preparations, a decorative and tasty treat. The wine list is limited. For dessert we chose a white chocolate-banana tart with Kahlúa cream and a pecan-ricotta strudel with caramel sauce.

Nine rooms, each with private bath. $135–$220. Breakfast and afternoon refreshment included. Children welcome. Third person $28. No smoking. No pets. Dinner served Wednesday through Saturday (also Sunday during the summer and foliage season), 5:30 to 9 P.M. Entrées $15–$18. Old Littleton Road, Bethlehem, NH 03574; (603) 444-2600, (888) 444-2600 fax (603) 444-4823; www.adairinn.com.

What to Do.   For walking in the area, cross the street to the 1,200-acre Rocks Estate. At 6,288 feet, Mount Washington is the highest point in the northeastern United States. If it's a clear day (about 50% of the time the mountain has a cloud cover), take the auto road to the top of Mount Washington (mid-May to mid-October). Or take the cog railway with the little coal-fired engines to the summit. Drive through Franconia Notch, walk through the Flume, and take the tramway up Cannon Mountain. Stop at the Appalachian Mountain Club information center at the old railroad station in Crawford Notch for detailed hiking information and maps. There's also a ranger station in Bethlehem at the edge of the 700,000-acre White Mountains National Forest. Downhill skiing is at Cannon, Bretton Woods, Loon, Attitash, and Wildcat. For cross-country skiing, go to Bretton Woods or Jackson. If you love to shop the outlets there's a 5-mile-long strip along Route 16 from Conway to North Conway. (NOTE: There is no sales tax in New Hampshire.)

How to Get There.   From I-93, take exit 40. Turn right at the exit and immediately turn left to the entrance drive of the inn.

The Notchland Inn

The Notchland Inn, *Harts Location, New Hampshire*

The location of this inn is truly spectacular. The secluded 1862 granite mansion sits on a 100-acre property in the midst of the White Mountains, a fairy-tale setting. You feel close to nature as you are totally surrounded by mountains with not another building visible in any direction. The inn has an informal rustic feel with a front parlor designed by Gustav Stickley, a prominent designer and furniture maker of the Arts and Crafts movement in the United States. Guests gather there by the fireplace or in the adjacent music room, where there are a piano, a stereo, and games. Combine the location with good dining and warm welcoming from innkeepers Ed Butler, a former health professional, and Les Schoof, formerly the general manager of the American Ballet Theatre in New York City, and you have a winner. Coco, their large lovable Bernese mountain dog, also adds to the welcome. Other animals on the property include a Belgian draft horse, two llamas, and two miniature horses.

After a day of hiking or skiing, a favorite activity is a soak in the wood-fired hot tub, which sits in the gazebo next to the pond (from which there's a great view of the mountains).

All the rooms and suites have queen-size or king-size beds and all have wood-burning fireplaces. The Carter Suite, the newest and the most popular, is located over the dining room. It has a bath with a whirlpool tub and a private deck with mountain views. A second new suite, also over the dining room, has an even more deluxe bath with a whirlpool tub as well as a separate shower. The Kinsman Suite has a king-size bed and a large living room with an exquisite Japanese wedding kimono mounted on the wall. The other accommodations in the main inn are rooms, all with fireplaces and views across the valley. The favorite rooms are the Crawford Room, the front corner room on the second floor, with a king-size bed, and the Franconia Room, the front corner room on the first floor, with a queen-size bed.

The Schoolhouse Building, behind the inn, has two suites. Dixville, the second-floor suite, is our favorite as it has a living room with a large arched window with a view of the valley and a bedroom with a queen-size bed.

Dinner is served at 7 P.M. at individual tables. Windows on one side of the dining room overlook the pond and the gazebo, while the other side has a view of the perennial gardens and the mountains. In this comfortable environment two soups, two appetizers, three entrées, salad, and three deserts are offered nightly. Vegetarian meals and special dietary restrictions may be accommodated with advance notice. You make your entrée choice when you sit down, but the soups, appetizers, and desserts are brought to the tables on a tray so you can decide on the spot which choice catches your fancy. The night we stayed we tried both the white bean and dill as well as the creamed broccoli and watercress soups. The second course choices were small pieces of puff pastry topped with mozzarella and sliced tomato and mussels broiled with garlic butter. Entrée choices were tender boneless rolled chicken with Brie and herbs, grilled shrimp, or a small steak served with mashed yams and spinach. From the rolling dessert cart we had the summer fruit pie and the white-and-dark-chocolate truffle cake. A tradition of the inn is seconds on dessert.

Twelve rooms and suites, each with private bath. $185–$230; foliage and holiday periods, $215–$270. Breakfast and dinner for two included. 15% gratuity. Bed-and-breakfast rates $40 less. Children over 12 welcome. Third person, $50 additional, including dinner. No smoking. No pets. Two-night weekend minimum. Hart's Location, NH 03812; (603) 374-6131, (800) 866-6131; fax (603) 374-6168; www.notchland.com.

What to Do.   You are in the middle of the White Mountain National Forest. There are limitless opportunities for hiking as the Davis Path to Mount Crawford starts across the road and close by are trails to Arethusa Falls and Frankenstein Cliffs. The inn has an 8,000-foot frontage on the Saco River, one of the best swimming holes in the area, and 2 miles of backcountry trails for cross-country skiing or snowshoeing (snowshoe rentals are available at the inn). You can take the cog railroad to the top of Mount Washington or drive around to the other side of the mountain and take the auto road to the summit. Drive through Crawford Notch to Franconia Notch with a stop at the Flume to take a walk through the gorge. Drive the Kancamagus Highway. The Crawford Notch Scenic Train runs through some of the most beautiful mountain scenery in the Northeast. There is an extensive system of cross-country trails around Jackson. Downhill ski areas within a ten-minute drive include Attitash and Bretton Woods. For shopping, head to the discount stores in North Conway.

How to Get There.   From Boston, take I-93 north to exit 35 (Route 3). Take Route 3 north to Route 302. Go east on Route 302 for 16.5 miles to the inn. From Hartford, take I-91 north to Wells River (exit 17). Follow Route 302 to I-93 (just before Littleton, N.H.) Take I-93 south to exit 40 (Bethlehem). Take Route 302 east through Crawford Notch.

The Inn at Thorn Hill

The Inn at Thorn Hill, *Jackson Village, New Hampshire*

This 1895 home designed by Stanford White is up the street from the center of Jackson Village. Innkeepers Jim and Ibby Cooper purchased the property in 1992 and since then have made it one of the top inns in the area with one of the best restaurants in the state.

The first floor includes two common rooms; a restaurant, bar, and lounge area with a television; and a wicker-filled front porch with views of the mountains. Room 1 has a carved Victorian mahogany queen-size bed, an antique brass twin bed, an Oriental rug, and a sink made from a village pulpit. Room 2 has a queen-size bed with a carved high headboard, a silk Oriental rug, the best view of the Presidential Mountains, and a bath with the sink in the room, set into a cherry dresser. The Katherine Suite, Room 5, popular with honeymooners, has a bedroom with a queen-size bed and a double whirlpool tub, a separate sitting room with a gas fireplace, and a newly redone bath with a shower. The Stanford Suite, Room 6, has a gas fireplace in the sitting room and stained-glass panels in the bathroom window and door. The Presidential Suite, Room 8, has a bath with a whirlpool tub next to the window with a view of Mount Washington, a sitting room with a gas fireplace and a wet bar, and a bedroom with a queen-size bed. Room 9 has views of the Iron Mountains, a king-size bed, and a gas fireplace.

The three cottages, certainly the most deluxe accommodations and perfect for guests seeking seclusion, were renovated and expanded. Each has a huge new bath with a double whirlpool tub and a separate shower as well as a gas fireplace. In Notch View there's a screened porch, a sitting room with a fireplace and a wet bar, and a separate bedroom with a queen-size bed. Forest View has a living room with a fireplace that is visible from the double whirlpool tub, steep stairs leading to a second-floor bedroom with a king-size bed and sloped ceiling with skylights, and a deck on the back of the cottage. Trailside is one large room with a peaked roof and carved queen-size bed, a deluxe bath with a view of the forest, and a deck with a view of the mountains.

The Carriage House has newly redone country-style rooms with knotty pine walls, a queen-size bed and a day bed, and a Great Room with a wood-burning fireplace, which makes it a particularly popular building in the winter. Rooms 14, 17, and 20 have single-size whirlpool tubs, and Room 16 has a double-size tub. Rooms 17 and 19 have wood ceilings that give them a warmer feel. There's a hot tub on the deck of this building and a large swimming pool adjacent to it.

A full breakfast, served from 8 to 9:30 A.M., includes a cold buffet of juices, fruit, cereals, and sweet breads. Entrées the day we stayed included delicious crispy French toast rolled in corn flakes and topped with blueberry plum sauce, and cheddar-and-tomato omelettes.

At dinner ask to sit in the larger of the two dining rooms. Appetizers on the July evening we dined included smoked swordfish samosa, a pan-fried pastry filled with grilled smoked swordfish, fresh artichokes, and oven-dried tomatoes; and chicken-and-Gorgonzola involtini, marinated herbed chicken and Gorgonzola cheese roasted in grape leaves and served with a sauce of wild mushrooms and roasted fresh tomatoes.

Entrées included a large portion of fresh linguine with calamari, mussels, and seared greens in a tomato curry sauce with pickled garlic and toasted cashews; grilled sirloin steak with a pepper pumpkin seed crust and a zinfandel-and-fresh tarragon sauce; and mahimahi served on mushroom polenta with a sun-dried-tomato-and-bacon cream sauce. The award-winning wine list is extensive and includes a special selection of wines chosen to complement the current menu. For dessert, chocolate lovers will go for the flourless chocolate cake. We had cappuccino bread pudding and ripe native strawberries with crème anglaise.

Sixteen rooms and suites, and three cottages. $160–$300. Breakfast and dinner for two included. 15% service charge.

Bed-and-breakfast rate $15 less per person. Children over 10 welcome. Third person $50 additional. No pets. No smoking. Two-night winter weekend minimum. Dinner nightly 6 to 9 P.M., except midweek in April. Thorn Hill Road, Box A, Jackson Village, NH 03846; (603) 383-4242, (800) 289-8990; fax (603) 383-8062; www.innatthornhill.com.

What to Do.   Walk down the hill to see the falls in the center of Jackson. Go to the top of Mount Washington by the auto road or the cog railroad. Pack a picnic lunch and take a hike. Take a drive through Crawford Notch to Franconia Notch with a stop at the Flume to take a walk through the gorge. Take the Kancamagus Highway. There is an extensive system of cross-country trails around Jackson. Downhill ski areas within a ten-minute drive include Wildcat, Attitash, and Cranmore. For shopping, head to the discount stores in North Conway.

How to Get There.   From Boston, take I-95 north to the Spaulding Turnpike and follow Route 16 north to Jackson. To avoid the traffic in North Conway, take West Side Road at the first light in Conway to River Road to Route 16. From Hartford, take I-84 to the Massachusetts Turnpike (I-90). Head east on Route 290 through Worcester. Take Route 495 north to I-95 to the Spaulding Turnpike. Then follow the above directions.

Nestlenook Farm

Nestlenook Farm, *Jackson Village, New Hampshire*

This deluxe Victorian bed-and-breakfast is located on sixty-five acres overlooking formal gardens, a heated swimming pool, a Victorian chapel, and a three-acre stocked trout pond. The inn's setting evokes images created by fairy tales. Guests can enjoy the luxury of a vast amount of private space whether they come in summer or winter. In winter, guests are transported to a Currier and Ives scene complete with horse-drawn sleigh rides, ice skating on the pond, and hot chocolate and cookies in the massive fireplaced gazebo. In the summer spend time in the hammocks by the swimming pool that has swim jets (to create a current) and relax on the electric massage bed. On a rainy day or in the evening head to the basement recreation room, where there is a billiard table, dart board, and state-of-the art surround-sound video system.

Nothing has been spared to make Nestlenook a showcase. It is lavishly decorated with coordinated designer fabrics and furnished with high-quality antiques. All of the rooms have phones, whirlpool tubs (five are double whirlpools), and one room has a wood-burning fireplace. The Murdoch and McConnell Suites have air-conditioning; the others have fans. The top choice is the third-floor Murdoch Suite, with a bath as big as a bedroom where you can lie in the double whirlpool and view the grounds. The sitting room has a daybed and two easy chairs, and the bedroom has a queen-size bed. The Horace Burdick Suite has a queen-size bed, a separate sitting room with a daybed, and a large bath with a double whirlpool. The king-size bed in the William Paskell Room faces the wood-burning fireplace, making this room a top choice for the winter.

Guests have access to a full kitchen. Wine and cheese are served in the afternoon, and in the evening you can munch fresh popcorn while you watch a movie in the recreation room. Breakfast includes fresh orange juice, fruit, cereals, and an entrée such as Belgian waffles with whipped cream and fruit, cinnamon French toast, or oven-baked omelettes.

Seven rooms and suites, each with private bath. Summer, $125–$230; winter, $175–299. Breakfast and hors d'oeuvres included. Sleigh rides, mountain bikes, ice skating, rowboats, and fishing included. 15% service charge. Children over 12 welcome. No pets. No smoking. Two-night weekend minimum. Dinsmore Road, Jackson Village, NH 03846; (603) 383-9443, (800) 659-9443; fax (603) 383-4515.

Where to Dine.   The best food in the area and an excellent wine list are found at the Inn at Thorn Hill (Thorn Hill Road, Jackson; (603) 383-4242). Grilled sirloin with a pumpkin seed crust and linguine topped with calamari and mussels are two favorites. At the Wildcat Tavern (Jackson Village, (603) 383-4245), an old rambling building with an atmospheric pub, for brunch try "the cholesterol killer" lobster Benedict or the plate of shrimp, lobster, and scallops served over a wild rice mixture. At the more casual Thompson House Eatery (Route 16 and 16A, Jackson Village; (603) 383-9341), the chicken San Remo—a mound of sautéed chicken, sweet peppers, onions, eggplant, and sun-dried tomatoes—as well as the meat loaf parmigiana, amply take care of hefty appetites. Large portions of aged sirloin steak, barbecued ribs, and prime rib pack in the crowds at the Red Parka Pub, a popular hangout (Route 302, Glen; (603) 383-344).

What to Do.   See the falls in the center of Jackson. Go to the top of Mount Washington by the auto road or the cog railroad. Pack a picnic lunch and take a hike. Take a drive through Crawford Notch to Franconia Notch with a stop at the Flume to take a walk through the gorge. The Crawford Notch Scenic Train runs through some of the most beautiful mountain scenery in the Northeast. Take the Kancamagus Highway. There is an extensive system of cross-country trails around Jackson. Downhill ski areas within a ten-minute drive include Wildcat, Attitash, and Cranmore. If you are the type to "shop till you drop," head to the five-mile-long strip of discount stores in North Conway.

How to Get There.   From Boston, take I-95 north to the Spaulding Turnpike and follow Route 16 north to Jackson. To avoid the traffic in North Conway, take West Side Road at the first light in Conway to River Road to Route 16. From Hartford, take I-84 to the Massachusetts Turnpike (I-90). Head east on Route 290 through Worcester. Take Route 495 north to I-95 to the Spaulding Turnpike. Then follow the above directions.

The Manor on Golden Pond

The Manor on Golden Pond, *Holderness, New Hampshire*

This deluxe 1907 inn on thirteen acres on a hill overlooking and fronting Squam Lake is just south of the White Mountains. It was built by a wealthy Englishman who brought top artisans and craftsmen from around the world to create a showplace. Since purchasing the property in 1992, innkeepers David and Bambi Arnold have upscaled the inn and totally redone every room with an individual decor, quality furnishings, and fine designer fabrics. Common areas include two sitting rooms, the Three Cocks Pub, and terraces set with lawn furniture. Facilities at the inn include a tennis court and a large swimming pool. The inn has three acres of frontage on Squam Lake, a small beach area, canoes, and a swimming raft.

Within the inn, ten of the seventeen rooms have wood-burning fireplaces; many also have private decks with lake views. All the rooms have televisions and air-conditioning, and many have mirrored walls that give the rooms a spacious feel. If a large whirlpool is high on your list of amenities, the three best rooms are Norfolk, Avon, and Wellington, each with an extra large double whirlpool tub in an alcove of the room, a king-size bed, a wood-burning fireplace, a private deck, and a separate bath with a shower. Bambi recently decorated Stratford Room to look like a trappers' lodge with a king-size canopy bed, fireplace, barnboard walls with mounted antlers, snowshoes, animal skins, and a bearskin rug. We loved it. Windsor, a second-floor corner room with large picture windows, fireplace, and queen-size four-poster bed, has the best panoramic view of the lake, but it doesn't have a deck. Especially large rooms with private decks with lake views and fireplaces include Churchill and Savoy Court, both with king-size beds.

Each accommodation in the Carriage House is a one-bedroom suite with a wood-burning fireplace and a refrigerator. Top choices are Berkshire, on the second floor with a double whirlpool tub and a private deck, and Ascot, on the first floor with a large stone fireplace.

The cottages are more rustic. These are the only accommodations where children are permitted. Two of the four two-bedroom cottages have fireplaces. The favorite (and most expensive) is Dover as it has a fireplace and is the only cottage next to the lake.

Breakfast for guests staying at the inn includes a cold buffet of juice, fruit salad, yogurt, and granola, as well as a different hot entrée each day such as buttermilk pancakes, French toast, or omelette of the day served with ham, bacon, or sausages.

Before dinner have a drink in the Three Cocks Pub, an intimate piano bar with small copper-topped tables and numerous decorative roosters.

Two dining rooms include the dark wood-paneled former billiard room with beamed ceiling and leaded windows and a second room adjacent to the pub that overlooks a terrace. The inn has an award-winning wine list. The leisurely five-course meal includes a choice of three appetizers and three desserts. The presentation of the plates is particularly attractive. The menu changes every night. Dinner might start with chilled carrot soup with pickled ginger followed by crispy skate with Thai sauce, rabbit-and-duck cassoulet, or layered phyllo with wild mushrooms. The salad also changes nightly. We had entrées of steamed mussels in flavorful broth with garlic bread and medium-rare sliced Magret duck breast. The third choice was a veal chop. The evening's dessert might be wine-poached pears with chocolate crème fraîche or strawberry sorbet with white chocolate mousse.

Twenty-one rooms and suites, each with private bath. $190–$325. Breakfast, afternoon tea, and dinner for two included. 15% service charge. Bed-and-breakfast rates available. Children over 12 welcome in the inn. Rooms are double occupancy only. No smoking. Country Cottages, four two-bedroom cottages with kitchens or kitchenettes. Weekly rental, $950–$1,750. Children welcome. No pets. Meals not included. Cottages and Carriage House open June through October. Dinner served nightly mid-June through October; other times of the year, Wednesday through Sunday. Prix fixe $50. Box T, Route 3, Holderness, NH 03245; (603) 968-3348, (800) 545-2141.

What to Do.   During the summer you can take a sightseeing boat around Squam Lake to see the sites featured in the film *On Golden Pond*. For shopping go to Tilton Mall, which has the same upscale outlet stores as in Conway. Visit the studio of Peppi Herman, a glassblower specializing in dishes and stemware. Quilting Keepsake, a large quilting mail-order company, has its company store nearby. Take a hike or visit the top of Mount Washington by the auto road or the cog railway. Other sights in the White Mountains include the Flume, the Aerial Tram at Cannon Mountain, and the gorge at Lost River. Winter visitors can enjoy five ski areas within thirty minutes, cross-country skiing, skating, and ice fishing.

How to Get There.   From Boston, take I-93 north to New Hampshire exit 24 (Ashland-Holderness). Bear right off the exit onto Route 3 south and proceed for 4.7 miles. From Hartford, take I-84 east to the Massachusetts Turnpike (I-90). Head east on Route 290 through Worcester. Proceed onto Route 495 north to I-93 north. Continue on I-93 to exit 24, then follow the above directions.

The Inn on the Common

The Inn on the Common, *Craftsbury Common, Vermont*

Craftsbury Common is a village of white clapboard homes in Vermont's pristine Northeast Kingdom. Since 1973 innkeepers Penny and Michael Schmitt have owned the inn, which now comprises three late-eighteenth-and nineteenth-century Federal-style buildings. The remoteness of the village and the serenity of the landscape contribute to the romantic feeling you get when you stay here. For those who are horticulturists, wine connoisseurs, or interested in Chinese porcelains this inn will have a particularly strong appeal. Penny has a great devotion to her extensive perennial gardens, where there's a continuing show of flowers throughout the season. One garden next to a newly built and landscaped five-bay pergola is pink in spring and, when the last tulip dies, changes to all white. There is also a swimming pool, an English croquet lawn, and a tennis court on the property. In the summer we like to sit out back in the Adirondack chairs overlooking the valley below and watch the sun set over distant Mount Mansfield. Some of the best cross-country skiing in the East is available here, as the inn is on the 110-kilometer trail system of the Craftsbury Nordic Ski Center. The area has almost a continuous snow cover during the winter months. In fact, the inn guarantees snow for skiing (January through mid-March) or you get your deposit back.

The first floor of the Main Building, built in 1795, has a library lounge that includes a well-equipped honor bar and shelves of all the proper size glasses from brandy snifters to Burgundy wineglasses, and a newly redecorated living room. Before dinner guests gather here for cocktails and hors d'oeuvres, and following dinner they retire to the two lounges for coffee and chocolates. A steep flight of stairs leads to the second floor, where there are five rooms.

The South Annex, across the street, has six rooms on two floors. The living room has a fireplace, a television with a VCR, and a collection of 250 movies. A number of our favorite deluxe rooms are in this building. Room 10 is the most requested as it has a particularly romantic feeling with a queen-size fishnet canopy bed and a couch in front of the fireplace stove. Room 7 is a two-bedroom suite with a master bedroom with a queen-size bed, a fireplace stove, and two easy chairs, and a second smaller bedroom with twin beds. Room 12, on the first floor, is a particularly spacious room with a king-size bed and a large bath.

The North Annex, about a quarter of a mile up the road just off the village common, is a five-bedroom house. Top choices here are Room 15, on the first floor, a large room with king/twin beds that face a fireplace and a small bath with a shower only. Room 16, on the second floor, has a queen-size canopy bed, a fireplace stove, and windows on three sides of the room. Note the wooden wine crates holding firewood in rooms with woodstoves or fireplaces.

Cocktails and hors d'oeuvres start at 6:30 P.M. At 7:30 guests are seated at three or four tables, or by request at individual tables, to enjoy a gourmet five-course candlelit dinner. The feeling is that of an elegant dinner party. Michael, who has a Wine Spectators Award of Excellence, continues to add to his connoisseur's wine list with many fine and very reasonably priced ready-to-drink Bordeaux, Burgundy, and California specialties. The menu changes nightly and typically includes a choice of two appetizers, two soups, two salads, four entrées, and three desserts. A recent menu included appetizers of a chèvre tart with caramelized onions or carpaccio of salmon with melon and asiago cheese. The soups were maple carrot with ginger or potato cheddar with scallions. Salads were three-bean served on mixed greens or spinach with egg, onions, and bacon. Entrées were roasted rack of lamb, cherry planked salmon, Thai coconut curried vegetables, or sautéed breast of duck. Dessert selections were white chocolate macadamia nut brownies with maple caramel sauce, amaretto cheesecake with fresh strawberries, or apple pie à la mode. Retire to the library for coffee, chocolates, and brandy.

A hearty breakfast, served from 8 to 9:30 A.M., includes a full menu with choices of entrées such as a custom omelette; a chef's special, which on the day we were there was baked stuffed potato with cheddar cheese and an egg; eggs any style; hot or cold cereals; and bacon, sausage, or Canadian bacon.

Sixteen rooms, each with private bath. $230–$250, foliage season, $270–$290. Breakfast and dinner for two included. Bed-and-breakfast rates $15 less per person. 15% service charge. Children welcome, $35–$65 (depending on age). Pets permitted, advance notice required; $15. Craftsbury Common,

VT 05827; (802) 586-9619, (800) 521-2333; fax (802) 586-2249; www.innonthecommon.com.

What to Do. The Craftsbury Nordic Ski Center (800) 729-7751) has 110 kilometers of groomed and tracked trails. You can leave from a trail at the inn or drive 2 miles to the center, where equipment can be rented and instruction arranged. In late March or April visit a sugarhouse and watch maple syrup being made. During the summer we suggest a drive on the scenic back roads that follow the ridges and afford spectacular views. Plan a loop with stops at the Cabot Creamery to watch cheese being made, at the Old Stone House Museum, a historical museum in Brownington Village, and at the museum of the internationally known Bread and Puppet theater troupe in Glover. Golfers can play in Greensboro, a walking course.

How to Get There. Take I-91 to St. Johnsbury. Take exit 21 to Route 2B to Route 2 west to Danville. Take Route 15 west to Hardwick. Take Route 14 north and bear right at the sign to Craftsbury Common.

Rabbit Hill Inn

Rabbit Hill Inn, *Lower Waterford, Vermont*

Tucked into a Vermont hillside near the Connecticut River is Lower Waterford, a thoroughly traditional New England village. The steepled church, stamp-size post office, library, and eighteenth-century houses all are painted white with dark green shutters. Within this storybook setting you'll find the utterly romantic Rabbit Hill Inn.

Hospitality, which is spelled here with a capital *H*, starts when you arrive in time for tea, served from 2:30 P.M. by owners Leslie and Brian Mulcahy. In winter you will find mulled cider, venison stew, or chili warming in the black kettle that hangs over the hearth in the tavern; in warm weather, sample homemade cookies and iced tea made from red clover, the state flower.

Choosing among the twenty rooms is difficult. Here are some of our favorites in the main house. The Loft, the largest room in the inn, has its own private staircase. Special features include a cathedral ceiling, hand-hewn beams, an eight-foot Palladian window, a king-size canopy bed, a fireplace with a couch and two rocking chairs, and a deck at the back of the inn. The bath has a double whirlpool and a separate shower. The Nest is a suite on the third floor with a wrought iron queen-size canopy bed that faces the fireplace and has a canopy that can be drawn completely around the bed, a sundeck, a large dressing room with a chaise longue and a mirrored vanity, and a bath with a double whirlpool tub and a separate shower. The spacious third-floor Cummings Suite has a living room with a fireplace, a bedroom, and a large private screened porch with a view of the White Mountains. The oversized Music Chamber Suite is equipped with a working pump organ, sheet music of the period, a Victrola, a collection of 78s, and a fainting couch, along with a king-size bed and a fireplace. In Victoria's Chamber, a king-size bed is framed with a blue demi canopy. There is a fireplace, a clothes tree hung with Victorian children's clothing, a Victorian couch, and the latest issue of *Victoria* magazine. The Canopy Room has a queen-size bed with an arched fishnet canopy facing a fireplace. Victoria's Chamber and the Canopy Room share a deck on the second floor.

The building next door is the 1795 Tavern Building. The Top of the Tavern Suite, on the top floor of the Tavern Building, has a large bedroom with a sitting area, a queen-size four-poster bed, and a fireplace, as well as a dressing room with a vanity, a daybed, and a collection of Victorian wardrobe accessories. The Turnabout, a handicap-accessible room, has a porch, a private outside entrance, a king-size canopy bed, a gas fireplace, and a bath with a double whirlpool tub. The Tavern Secret has a king-size fishnet canopy bed, a fireplace, a bookcase wall with a secret door that opens into a large bath with a double whirlpool and a separate shower.

Prior to dinner you will find Brian tending bar and conversing with guests in the tavern, which has a fireplace, couches, and easy chairs, or in the adjoining Irish pub, a separate room with hand-crafted tables and chairs.

Dining at the Rabbit Hill Inn is a creative and well-orchestrated culinary experience. Background music is provided by an accomplished guitarist. "Rabbity" touches are discreetly present in the butter molds, napkin rings, and porcelain table decorations. It is this attention to detail that sets Rabbit Hill apart from many other inns.

The five-course dinner includes choices at each course and changes seasonally. Appetizers from the midwinter menu included grilled duck sausage with cherries, pistachios, and foie gras; artichoke and cilantro pasta cake with a yogurt dressing; and smoked salmon and sweet potato gratin with roasted red peppers and portabello mushrooms. A choice of salads included Asian noodle salad, a salad of baby greens, or a classic Caesar salad. A taste of citrus champagne sorbet followed.

Entrées, a selection of about eight, included grilled duck breast with Chinese spices served with apricot wild rice bread pudding; spinach-ricotta tortellini in a Parmesan-and-basil cream sauce served with grilled foccacia; braised venison shank with wild mushrooms and gold potatoes; and tenderloin of beef with grilled grits with goat cheese and fried green peas.

For dessert we've had thin Hungarian pancakes filled with chopped hazelnuts and covered with peaches and strawberries with a caramel sauce, and frozen chocolate mousse cake with layers of mocha, white chocolate, and dark chocolate topped with hot fudge and whipped cream.

After an excellent evening meal, return to your room to find it lit by the glow of a candle, soft music playing, the bed turned down with flower petals strewn on the sheets, and a one-of-a-kind Do Not Disturb sign: a lacy heart-shaped pillow, the Mulcahys' gift to you.

Rise in the morning to a generous breakfast: juice, muffins or other sweet breads, homemade granola, a fruit course, and a choice of two entrées. We had soufflé French toast with heart-shaped molds of butter and Vermont maple syrup.

Twenty-one rooms and suites, each with private bath. $199–$289. Full breakfast, afternoon tea, and dinner included. 15% service charge. Children over 12 welcome. Third person $70 additional. No pets. No smoking. Two-night minimum on weekends. Dinner served nightly. Prix fixe $37. A limited number of dinner reservations are accepted for guests not staying at the inn. Route 18, Lower Waterford, VT 05848; (802) 748-5168, (800) 76-BUNNY; fax (802) 748-8342; www.rabbithill.com.

What to Do.   The inn has a swimming pond, gazebo, and hiking trails. Backroading, antiquing, cross-country skiing, downhill skiing, and canoeing are all available in the area; for golfers, the inn has a membership at a nearby club. Visit the St. Johnsbury Athenaeum's art gallery to see the ten-by-fifteen-foot *Domes of the Yosemite*, by Albert Bierstadt, and other paintings displayed at the gallery at the back of the library. Take a driving tour of the White Mountains in New Hampshire. If it's a clear day, drive to the top of Mount Washington or take the cog railway to the summit. Drive through Franconia Notch, walk through the Flume, and take the tramway up Cannon Mountain. Stop at the Appalachian Mountain Club at Pinkham Notch for detailed hiking information and maps.

How to Get There.   From Boston, take I-93 north to exit 44 onto Route 18 north, 2 miles to the inn. From Hartford, take I-91 north to exit 19 to I-93 south. Take exit 1 onto Route 18 south, 7 miles to the inn.

The Inn at the Round Barn Farm

The Inn at the Round Barn Farm,
Waitsfield, Vermont

Surrounded by pastures, lush green hills, the silos of Vermont hill farms, and an outdoor sculpture garden, this deluxe inn set on eighty-five acres was a working dairy farm until the 1960s. The nineteenth-century farmhouse and attached horse barn were converted to guest rooms, common spaces, and a cross-country ski center by Jack and Doreen Simko and their daughter AnneMarie DeFreest. The adjacent round barn, built in 1910, was restored by the Simkos and is used for community activities, weddings, concerts, conferences, and art exhibits throughout the year. The lower level of the barn is a sixty-foot lap pool that extends into a greenhouse and doubles as the water source for the inn's sprinkler system. In order to protect the beautiful hardwood floors, guests (who come in the winter) leave their shoes under the entranceway bench and put on a pair of slippers that the inn provides. The first floor of the inn includes a library with a wood-burning fireplace, a good selection of coffee table books about Vermont, and a decanter of sherry. There's also a lower-level game room with an antique pool table, an organ, a television with a VCR and a collection of movies, a refrigerator stocked with complimentary juices and soda, games, and lots of paperback books.

The new luxury rooms on the second floor of the attached barn are our favorites. These four spacious rooms have the original high-peaked roof rafters and barnboard ceilings, gas fireplaces, paddle fans, and air-conditioners. The largest and most sumptuous is the Richardson Room, with a king-size bed with a matching fabric-covered headboard and half-canopy, a couch, and a chaise longue by the fireplace. Built-in cherry cabinetry separates the bedroom from the bath area, which has a double whirlpool tub with a skylight next to low windows, a perfect spot for looking at the hills. A separate shower with glass on two sides and a private toilet alcove complete this large room. The Sherman Room has a queen-size mahogany sleigh bed, wingback chairs by the fireplace, and three Winslow Homer drawings from an 1870 issue of *Harper's Weekly* hanging on the walls. The bathroom has a large pedestal sink and a steam shower (very relaxing after skiing). The Dana Room is very romantic, with a queen-size bed with a white chiffon canopy, a fainting couch, and a bath with a steam shower. The English Room has king/twin beds with matching yellow floral wallpaper and bedspread and a bath with a steam shower.

There are two rooms on the first floor. The Joslin Room is a corner room with a king-size canopy bed, a gas fireplace, and fine antiques including a highboy, an Oriental carpet, and a ladies' secretary. The bath was expanded and now includes a double whirlpool tub with a waterfall faucet and a steam shower. The former sunporch breakfast room is now the Sterling Room, a very bright room with a queen-size bed and a gas fireplace.

Breakfast is served from 8:15 to 9:30 A.M. in a large room with hand-hewn beams and windows on both sides with a view of the hills. The room is arranged with a number of tables, allowing guests to eat by themselves or with others. Breakfast includes juice, fresh fruit, muffins, and a hot entrée such as egg strata or blueberry waffles—or if you prefer, hot or cold cereal with fruit. A buffet dinner is served on Friday nights in the winter.

Eleven rooms, each with private bath. December to early April, $135–250; other times, $135–$220. Foliage season and holidays $20 additional. Afternoon refreshment and breakfast included. Children over 15 welcome. Third person in the Terrace Room $25 additional. Other rooms are double occupancy only. No pets. No smoking. Two-night weekend minimum. RR1, Box 247, East Warren Road, Waitsfield, VT 05673; (802) 496-2276; fax (802) 496-8832; www.innattheroundbarn.com.

Where to Dine. The Common Man (802) 583-2800) serves a continental menu in an atmospheric old barn with a stone fireplace. Chez Henri (802) 583-2600) is a French bistro. Giorgio's Café (802) 496-3983) specializes in Italian. The Lareau Farm (802) 496-8856) serves flatbread with creative toppings cooked in a wood-fired oven. John Egan's Big World Pub (802) 496-3033) is a local place with excellent fare but no atmosphere. And for Chinese go to China Moon (802) 583-6666).

What to Do. Winter activities could include a romantic sleigh ride for two, or cross-country skiing or snowshoeing on the inn's thirty kilometers of groomed and tracked trails with the latest state-of-the-art equipment. For downhill skiing go to Sugar Bush and Mad River Glen. For a summer stay go hiking, canoeing on the Mad River, mountain biking, or horseback riding on Icelandic horses. For day trips visit Shelburne Museum to see the 200,000, piece collection of American; the Ben & Jerry's ice cream factory in Waterbury; Stowe, where you can drive to the top of Mount Mansfield; or Middlebury, to shop at Fox Hollow for outstanding Vermont crafts. Special activities at the Round Barn include a Sunday evening summer concert series and a juried Vermont craft show in mid-September to mid-October.

How to Get There.   Take I-89 to Middlesex, exit 9. Go south on Route 100B to Route 100 south. In Waitsfield, turn left at Bridge Street, go through the covered bridge and bear right at the fork onto East Warren Road. The inn is 1 mile down the road on the left.

Woods Cottage at Twin Farms

Twin Farms, *Barnard, Vermont*

This 240-acre grand estate north of Woodstock was recently transformed into one of the finest hideaways that we have ever seen. The farmhouse was Dorothy and Sinclair Lewis's country home in the 1930s and 1940s. Owner Thurston Twigg-

Smith spent millions of dollars renovating, putting in additions and new buildings, and doing an incredible job of decorating. Stunning pieces of art and antiques from his personal collection were combined to create a refined, quietly elegant, and unpretentious atmosphere.

When you come you are treated as a houseguest. There is no formal lobby, no reception desk, and no additional charges for any activity or for alcoholic beverages. The price is unquestionably high, but we feel that it is worth it if you are looking for this kind of exclusive retreat. There is a tremendous amount of common space spread among a number of buildings. The main house has a two-story central living room with an oversize fireplace, a huge window with a panoramic view, and a balcony library nook with CDs and videos. A second living room and a game room each have a fireplace, and there is an open bar for guests to help themselves at any time. Cross a footbridge to the ultramodern pub with a Wurlitzer jukebox that plays CDs, a forty-six-inch television, a pool table, a dart board, a fully stocked bar, glove-soft leather couches, and showcases filled with the owner's collection of beer bottles. A fitness center that rivals any that we have used in deluxe hotels is underneath this adult playground. After exercising cross the road to a building with a Japanese *furo*, a soaking tub. There are also a private ski slope and tow, a swimming and stocked fishing pond with canoes and rowboats, tennis courts, and miles of hiking trails.

Each accommodation has a wood-burning fireplace with a comfortable seating area and a large bath with a separate oversize shower and a tub. The cottages set in the woods are the most deluxe—and, if price is not a consideration, are our favorites. We stayed in the Treehouse, a cottage with a high-ceilinged main room with a latticework of birch logs around the vaulted ceiling, an ebonized four-poster king-size bed, a fireplace and sitting area, and a screened porch. The bath includes a whirlpool tub, double sinks, a separate toilet room with a bidet, and a slate-tiled shower with a heated floor.

The Perch Cottage, also surrounded by trees, is decorated with a fishing theme. It also has a king-size bed, a fireplace, a porch sitting room with wicker furniture, and a fabulous copper custom 300-gallon tub that is so large that you can float without touching the sides.

The Studio, a new two-story stone building, is the ultimate. It has a more formal feel with white plush carpeting, white couches, a Frank Stella painting over the fireplace, and a double-story cathedral ceiling. A screened porch has a large hot tub with views of the woods. The bedroom on the second floor has a king-size bed, a second fireplace, and a bath that also has a copper-lined 300-gallon tub.

Five newer cottages are the latest additions to this property. The Woods has sandstone floors from Tuscany, a fireplace in the outside porch room, a second fireplace in the bedroom, and a bathroom that opens onto a terrace in the woods. The Barn has a cathedral ceiling, a twenty-foot window with a view of the meadows, a loft lounge, a double-sided fireplace visible from the living room and the bedroom, and a heated screened porch. The Orchard has light-colored ash wood sliding panels in place of draperies that open to a wall of windows overlooking a beaver pond, a porch with a swing, a bedroom with a low platform bed, and a bath with a deep tub with a view of the orchard. The Log Cabin, a 250-year-old reconstructed Appalachian cabin decorated around the theme of dogs, has a living room with a cathedral ceiling and a large screened porch with a view of the forest. Meadow has an exotic Moroccan theme with a tented ceiling and a view of the meadow.

There are four rooms in the Main House. The Washington Room, a two-room first-floor suite with fireplaces in both rooms, decorated with an Americana theme, is a favorite.

There are two rooms in the Lodge, each with a private entrance with views and outdoor sitting areas that overlook the wildflower meadow and the ski slope. Beverley and Shaun Matthews, a British husband-and-wife team, are the general managers. They graciously act as host and hostess of this very special place.

Meals are served in a dining room that reminded us of a small European castle, with a large fieldstone Rumford fireplace at each end of the high arched room. Guests have their own table and are served a set gourmet lunch and dinner paired with wines, though individual requests or diets can be accommodated with no problem. Intimate dinners in the wine cellar, in the small dining room, or in your room can easily be arranged.

When we stayed one night's dinner included lobster consommé with lobster pieces and quail eggs served with Stags Leap Sauvignon Blanc; ricotta and saffron ravioli; an entrée of a trio of fish: poached salmon on shredded leeks, scallops on wilted greens, and tuna separated by piped potatoes served with baby turnips and carrots and paired with Acacia Chardonnay. Dessert was a caramel pot de crème surrounded by a painted plate with five sauces.

You can have a breakfast basket delivered to your room or you can come to the main house. You are also welcome to visit with the chef, Neil Wigglesworth, in his state-of-the-art kitchen at any time. We mentioned crêpes for breakfast and out came thin crêpes with lobster, goat cheese, and wild mushrooms in a light cream sauce—pure delight. Homemade sausage, blueberry pancakes, eggs Benedict or salmon Benedict, fresh-squeezed orange juice, and a basket of brioche, chocolate and plain croissants, and other sweet breads always come with breakfast. If it's late afternoon and you're ready for a cup of tea, finger sandwiches, and sweets, just let someone know. It's very easy to get awfully spoiled when you stay here.

Fourteen suites and cottages. $800–$1,500. 15% service charge additional. Breakfast, lunch, dinner, alcoholic beverages, and all activities and equipment are included. Closed in April. Not appropriate for children under 18. No pets. Barnard, VT 05031; (802) 234-9999, (800) TWIN-FARMS; fax (802) 234-9990.

What to Do. The historic character of Woodstock has been lovingly preserved. Its classic green is surrounded by examples of Georgian and Federal architecture. Four of the town's churches still ring bells cast by Paul Revere. Shoppers will enjoy browsing through the antiques shops, galleries, and upscale stores in town. Visit the Billings Farm Museum, where you can trace the daily life of a Vermont family hill farm in 1890. Visit the Simon Pearce Glass Mill in Quechee and watch glassblowers make the same glasses that are used at Twin Farms.

How to Get There. From Hartford, take I-91 to Route 12 to Route 4 west to Woodstock. From Boston, take I-89 to exit 1, left on Route 4 to Woodstock. In Woodstock, take Route 12 north to Barnard. Turn right at the general store for 1.5 miles to the stone pillar entrance on your right.

Red Clover Inn

Red Clover Inn, *Mendon, Vermont*

The attraction of this inn on thirteen acres located midway between Killington and Rutland on a quiet road off Route 4 is a combination of setting, new luxury rooms, an excellent restaurant, good wines, and the personal attention and enthusiasm of innkeepers Sue and Harris Zuckerman. The main inn includes three dining rooms; the Keeping Room, with a fieldstone fireplace, sofas, easy chairs, and plenty of games and magazines; and seven rooms on the second floor. The Carriage House and the recently completed addition to this building have seven rooms. There are also a pool, four miniature horses, and Lily, a lovable English bulldog.

The three newest deluxe rooms are in the Carriage House. Country Crossing, on the second floor, is our top favorite as it is the largest room and has a cathedral ceiling, a deck with great views, a massive four-poster pine king-size bed, a gas fireplace, and a double whirlpool tub in the room with a sky-light and a view of the fireplace. Mountain Retreat is a spacious first-floor corner room with a view of Pico Mountain, a king-size cherry bed, a gas fireplace, a double whirlpool tub in the bedroom, and a bath with an oversize shower. Garden Gables, next door, is similarly appointed. Carriage King, a deluxe room at the other end of this building, has a fireplace and a king-size bed. All of the deluxe rooms in the Carriage House and two of the three standard "dog-friendly" rooms in this building have televisions and most have VCRs.

One of the two deluxe rooms in the main inn is the Mountain Suite, with windows on three sides with a view of Pico Mountain, a queen-size bed, a gas fireplace, and a double whirlpool tub in the bedroom. Trillium, the other favorite, is a corner room with a Vermont-made black pencil-post queen-size bed facing a gas fireplace, a matching bureau, and a bath with a single-size whirlpool tub. A lower-priced favorite is Room 1, with mountain views from the queen-size bed.

Dinner was exceptional and is all-inclusive for guests. This means you can have any appetizer, a green salad, any entrée (including rack of lamb, the most expensive), and dessert. For appetizers we had delicate gingered pork dumplings served on a black octagonal plate with a garlic dipping sauce, and risotto flavored with baby shrimp, butternut squash, and pearl onions. For one entrée we had a superb rack of lamb, a portion of eight well-trimmed chops with a rosemary balsamic reduction and barley pilaf. We also had pan-roasted Vermont quail with wild mushrooms served with a potato, butternut squash, and parsnip ragout. Other choices included filet of beef, salmon crusted with pistachio nuts, and pork tenderloin glazed with cider. Every night the chef prepares a vegetarian entrée such as portabello strata with smoked tomato sauce or fusilli with grilled eggplant, sun-dried tomatoes, pignoli nuts, spinach, and Vermont feta cheese.

The excellent wine list includes understandable descriptions for many of the wines. Harris prints wine suggestions to go with the dinner, has discounted wine specials each week, and can't wait to show off his wine cellar to any interested diners. You can have a look at the entire wine list and dinner menu on their web site: redcloverinn.com.

For dessert we had the ravioli, an imaginative dish of white chocolate filled with chocolate ganache that looked like the real thing. For a lighter dessert we enjoyed the apple-pear strudel topped with crème anglaise and maple caramel sauce.

Breakfast, served from 8:30 to 9:30 A.M. at individual tables, includes a fruit plate, juice, and a platter for a couple to share such as French toast made with English muffin and cinnamon swirl bread, waffles topped with different fruits, vegetarian and cheese omelettes, lemon ricotta, and Swedish oatmeal pancakes with bacon and local sausage.

Fourteen rooms, each with private bath. Foliage, holidays, and winter, $165–$350; summer, $140–$250. Breakfast and dinner for two included. 15% service charge. Bed-and-breakfast rates available. Dinner not served on Sunday. Children over 10 welcome. Third person in selected rooms $60 additional, including dinner. No smoking. Pets permitted in three rooms. Two-night weekend minimum. 7 Woodward Road, Mendon, VT 05701; (802) 775-2290, (800) 752-0571; fax (802) 773-0594 www.redcloverinn.com.

What to Do. Visit the galleries and shops in Woodstock, an idyllic New England town. The Vermont Raptor Center and Billings Farm Museum, a nineteenth-century working farm and museum, are also in Woodstock. In Quechee you can watch the glassblowers at Simon Pearce Glass. Take a scenic drive to Middlebury and visit Frog Hollow, the Vermont state craft center. For outlet shopping go to Manchester. For downhill skiing go to Killington (5 miles) and Pico (3 miles). For cross-country skiing go to Mountain Meadows or Mountain Top, both about fifteen minutes away. In the summer go hiking on the Long Trail and the Appalachian Trail, go mountain biking on the trails at Killington, or bike or drive along the back roads.

How to Get There.   From New York, take the New York Thruway (I-87) north to Route 149 east to Route 4 east. Continue on Route 4 5.2 miles east of Rutland to a right on Woodward Road. Or take I-91 north to I-89 to Route 4 west (exit 1 in Vermont). Take Route 4 west to Mendon (3 miles beyond Pico). Turn left on Woodward Road.

The Jackson House Inn

The Jackson House Inn, *Woodstock, Vermont*

The Jackson House, set on a landscaped five-acre parcel, formerly a fine bed-and-breakfast inn, is now an even more deluxe property that includes a fine dining restaurant. In 1996 Juan and Gloria Florin purchased the inn along with the fine antiques, many of museum quality. The Florins have added two wings, one with four deluxe one-room suites and the other with the restaurant, both so well designed that it is difficult to tell the old from the new. The manicured gardens include an English garden, a stream with an arched bridge, a pond, and an expansive lawn with hammocks and chairs. Matt and Jennifer Barba are the resident innkeepers.

A lumber merchant built the house in 1890 using the finest craftsmen and woods available, which explains the floors of oak, cherry, and walnut, as well as the polished cherry staircase. The bedrooms and suites are furnished with exquisite period antiques. Even though the inn attracts outside diners, overnight guests have the exclusive use of the formal parlor, which has a woodstove, and the library. Continuing the tradition of the former owners, each evening from 6 to 7 P.M. houseguests are served complimentary white wine, champagne, local beer, and mineral water as well as fancy hors d'oeuvres such as smoked salmon, nori rolls, and foie gras.

Our favorite accommodations are the one-room suites, which include two on the third floor of the main inn as well as four new suites in the addition, each with a gas fireplace, a phone, and a stereo with a CD player. Nicholas and Francesca, the two suites on the third floor of the older section, are particularly popular in the warmer weather as they have French doors opening onto decks with great views of the grounds. Each has a queen-size cherry sleigh bed, a sitting area, and a marble-tiled bath with a shower only. The four new suites, accessed by a door off the front porch, are spacious rooms with queen-size beds, Anichini linens and fabrics, European-style down duvets, a sitting area, and luxurious baths with showers and separate tubs. The first-floor rooms are Wales Johnson, with a single-size whirlpool tub, and Christine Jackson, with a double-size thermal massage tub (with gentle air bubbles). Both have French doors opening onto a brick patio that leads out to the garden. The second-floor rooms are Malena's Tango, with a black iron bed and antique French tapestry chairs, and Clara's Corner, with a four-poster Sheraton bed. Both have large baths with skylights over the tubs, separate showers, and double-size thermal massage tubs.

The other nine, more moderately priced rooms, have small baths, all with showers with glass doors. Cranberry Room, a favorite on the first floor, has mauve silk wallcovering and French doors opening to the gardens. Second-floor favorites are Mary Todd Lincoln, with a Victorian bed; Gloria Swanson, with a tiger-and-bird's-eye maple bed; Governor Converse, with an 1860 cannonball bed; and Thorn Birds, with a brass-and-iron bed and a view of the gardens. The three New England–style rooms have fine furnishings but are slightly smaller with lower angled ceilings. A well-equipped exercise room with a large-screen television, a steam room, a universal gym, exercise machines, and a juice bar are in the basement.

Depending on the number of guests staying at the inn, breakfast (8 to 9:30 A.M.) is served either in the breakfast room with guests sitting around a large table or in the restaurant at individual tables overlooking the garden. The night we stayed the choices were delicious blueberry pancakes and bacon, oatmeal, or granola.

This is the top restaurant in Woodstock, so be sure to make dinner reservations before you arrive. The peaked high-ceilinged airy room is magnificent; it has well-spaced linen-draped tables, an especially large picture window that overlooks the gardens, smaller windows on the sides, and a stacked-stone double-sided wood-burning fireplace extending all the way to the high ceiling. The prix fixe dinner also includes an *amuse bouche*, sorbet, and choice of any appetizer, main course, and dessert. In addition there's a chef's tasting menu and a chef's vegetable menu that changes nightly. We had a superb meal starting with appetizers of grilled Maine sea scallops with chanterelles and sweet potato as well as Wellfleet oysters. For our main course one of us had a filet of beef with wild mushroom strudel, rosti potato cake, and grilled asparagus, and the other had sesame-crusted monkfish topped with a piece of lobster with quinoa pilaf. For dessert we indulged ourselves with the ice cream sandwich, made with flourless chocolate cake, homemade coconut ice cream, and chocolate sauce.

Nine rooms and six suites, each with private bath. Rooms, $170–$190; one-room suites, $240–$260. Hors d'oeuvres and breakfast included. Children over 14 welcome. Rooms are double occupancy only. No smoking. No pets. Two-night weekend minimum. Dinner served Thursday through Monday at most times of the year. Prix fixe $45–$55. Route 4 West, Woodstock, VT 05091; (802) 457-2065, (800) 448-1890; fax (802) 457-9290; www.jacksonhouse.com.

What to Do.   Visit the galleries and shops in Woodstock, an idyllic and historic New England town. Its classic green is surrounded by examples of Georgian and Federal architecture. The Vermont Raptor Center takes care of injured birds of prey that can't be released into the wild. Billings Farm Museum, a nineteenth-century working farm and museum, traces the daily life of a Vermont farm family. In Quechee you can watch the glassblowers at Simon Pearce Glass and watch the potters at work. A large retail shop has first-and second-quality merchandise. In Plymouth tour the village, which includes the Calvin Coolidge Homestead and the Plymouth Cheese Company, which makes excellent cheddar cheese. For downhill skiing go to Killington, Pico, or Suicide Six, a smaller ski area. For cross-country skiing go to the Woodstock Ski Touring Center.

How to Get There.   From Boston, take I-93 to I-89 to Route 4 west (exit 1 in Vermont). From New York, take the New York Thruway (I-87) north to Route 149 east to Route 4 east or I-95 to I-91 to Route 12 (exit 9) to Route 4 west. The inn is located on Route 4, 1.5 miles west of the village green.

Juniper Hill Inn

Juniper Hill, *Windsor, Vermont*

As you make the last turn up the country road, the sight of this imposing mansion on the hillside takes you by surprise. You enter through the Great Hall, a thirty-by-forty-foot central sitting room with English golden oak paneling. Off this room are two dining rooms, another sitting room with a fireplace, and a gentleman's library study. There is a terrace, a rolling lawn with well-tended perennial borders, and a swimming pool. The innkeepers are Susanne and Rob Pearl, who purchased the inn in July 1992.

Room 1, the largest, is a corner room with a spectacular sunrise view of the mountains. Both the queen-size canopy bed and the sofa face the wood-burning fireplace. Room 4, at the opposite corner of the second floor, has mountain views, a Charleston Rice four-poster queen-size bed and a sofa that faces the fireplace. Room 7, another newly redone room, has a queen-size bed with a seven-foot-high headboard facing the fireplace plus a twin bed, and is also a favorite. Room 2, with a light and airy floral decor, and Room 3, with a stenciled country motif, are smaller center rooms on the second floor that overlook the perennial gardens and the mountains.

For extra privacy we like Rooms 20 and 21, which are in a separate wing of the house over the library. Room 20, with a Franklin open-front woodstove, a queen-size bed, and a bath with an old-fashioned extradeep clawfoot tub, has a private porch with a pillowed chaise longue, a table, and chairs. Room 21, also with a woodstove, has a queen-size canopy bed. All nine rooms on the second floor have wood-burning fireplaces. The third-floor rooms all have high ceilings, and two of them, newly redecorated Rooms 16 and 17, have gas fireplaces.

Guests can have dinner at the inn; the menu of three entrées changes nightly but always includes one poultry, one fish, and one red meat entrée. Vegetarian meals are available with advance notice. The night we stayed the first course was mushroom leek soup. Other nights it could be an appetizer such as fresh spinach and feta cheese in phyllo dough or a three-cheese pizza with pesto. The salad course might be Caesar, mixed greens, or fresh pears, walnuts, and goat cheese on a bed of greens. Entrée choices the night we dined were poached salmon with a dill-and-caper sauce, grilled chicken breast topped with pesto, and charbroiled filet mignon with béarnaise sauce. Herb-crusted rack of lamb is another favorite. Desserts frequently served include peach bread pudding with warm caramel sauce, chocolate raspberry truffle cheesecake, and Swedish crème in puff pastry with a seasonal fruit sauce. After a day of touring we enjoyed a nice wine and the relaxing candlelit atmosphere of the dining room.

Breakfast, served from 8 to 9:30 A.M., includes choices of a hot dish (poached, fried, or scrambled eggs); two or three types of fruit-filled pancakes; French toast; and a daily special such as French toast stuffed with cream cheese and honey nuts and topped with fresh peaches, eggs Benedict, or grilled tomatoes topped with poached eggs and melted Vermont cheddar. You can also have breakfast in bed ($12 for two), which also includes a champagne cocktail.

Sixteen rooms, each with private bath, eleven with fireplace. $90–$150. Full breakfast and afternoon refreshment included. Children over 12 welcome. Third person $25 additional. No pets. No smoking. Dinner available Monday through Saturday by reservation. $28–$30. RR1, Box 79, Juniper Hill Road, Windsor, VT 05089; (802) 674-5273, (800) 359-2541; fax (802) 674-2041; www.juniperhillinn.com.

What to Do.   Drive north on Route 5 a couple of miles to the famous Simon Pearce glass-manufacturing facility and retail shop, where you can see the glassblowers working in teams hand blowing and finishing the pieces and potters working in the new pottery. At Catamount's Brewery, in Windsor, you can take a tour and visit their tasting room.

In Windsor visit the Vermont State Craft Gallery with crafts by more than 200 Vermont artisans. At the American Precision Museum you'll see machine tools, many displayed with the products they were used to make—rifles, sewing machines, typewriters, steam engines, coffee percolators, even a Model T. Drive across the Connecticut River on the 460-foot Windsor-Cornish Covered Bridge, the longest in the United States. In summer and fall continue to the Saint Gaudens National Historic Site to see how the first major American sculptor tossed away classical robes and dressed his subjects in current fashions. Visit the classic college town of Hanover, New Hampshire, home of Dartmouth College. Visit Woodstock, a picture-perfect New England town with its many shops and galleries.

How to Get There. From the south: Take exit 8 off I-91, then proceed north on Route 5 for about 6 miles to Windsor. Go through town and turn left on Juniper Hill Road (.25 mile past the shopping plaza). Proceed .5 mile up hill (bearing left at the fork) to driveway on right at crest of hill. From the north: Take exit 9 off I-91, then proceed south on Route 5 for 2.7 miles toward Windsor. Turn right on Juniper Hill Road, then follow above directions. By train: Amtrak stops in Windsor.

The Meadowlook Room at Windham Hill Inn

Windham Hill Inn, *West Townshend, Vermont*

Grigs and Pat Markham are the owners of this inn, located on 160 acres and ideally suited for those who appreciate nature and who want a quiet and peaceful getaway, deluxe rooms, and fine gourmet dining. There are enough magnificent panoramic views from the inn and ski and hiking trails to last your entire stay.

Accommodations are in the main inn building and the restored and refurbished White Barn, all with phones and air-conditioning. Since 1993 all the rooms have been renovated and numerous new ones have been constructed in the barn. The most deluxe are the three Loft Rooms, located on the second floor of the barn, each with a king-size canopy bed, a gas fireplace, and a large private deck. The largest is Meadowlook, twenty-three feet by twenty-six feet, with a large soaking tub in the room and a raised-hearth fieldstone fireplace. The Marion Goodfellow Room includes stairs leading to the cupola, which has a window seat and panoramic views in all directions. The North Loft has a fabulous bath with a double whirlpool tub next to windows overlooking the grounds. The first floor of the barn has five rooms. We like the view from the deck of the Matilda Hill Lawrence Room, a corner room with a queen-size sleigh bed, a gas stove, a barnboard ceiling, and a deck. William's Room is next door with a king-size bed, a gas stove, and a deck. General Fletcher has windows giving a fabulous view down the valley, a deck, and a gas stove. The Taft Suite, a handicap-accessible room, is an especially large room with a raised-hearth fireplace, a king-size bed, and a nine-foot window seat with a good view.

In the main building, we like Tree House, a smaller room with a queen-size canopy bed and a shaded porch where you can see the sun rise and where you feel like you're in the trees. Jesse Lawrence, a third-floor room, is very spacious with a king-size bed, a sitting area, a Vermont Castings stove, a soaking tub, and a separate shower. Other top choices are Robyn Whitney, with a double whirlpool tub and a fireplace, and Forget-Me-Not, with a soaking tub and a fireplace.

Guests gather in the Music Room, which opens out onto the back deck, or in the sitting room, with a fireplace for drinks and hors d'oeuvres followed by dinner (seatings at 6 to 6:45 or 8 to 8:30 P.M.). The inn's chef is outstanding. A five-course dinner includes a choice of three appetizers, soup, salad, a choice of four entrées, and five dessert choices. A sample winter menu includes appetizers of wild mushroom ravioli and grilled quail. Entrée choices are beef tenderloin with a Cabernet sauce, arctic char served in a light broth, and a phyllo cannelloni filled with tomatoes, spinach, eggplant, and bean curd. Dessert options were a warm chocolate mousse cake with bananas, poached pear with pistachio mousseline, lemon gratin with raspberry compote or fresh fruit, or sorbet.

Breakfast, served between 8 and 9:30 A.M., includes fresh squeezed orange juice, a fruit cup, granola, and a hot dish such as silver-dollar-size griddle cakes, fried eggs, and sausage or cinnamon brioche French toast with apple cranberry compote. A real nice touch is that while you're at breakfast the efficient staff will have your room cleaned and made up.

Hike on the inn's trails down to the beautiful waterfall and pools that reminded us of an Ansel Adams photograph—water flowing over the moss and ferns growing out of the rocks. If it's a warm day wear your bathing suit and take a dip. There are also a pool surrounded by a deck made of old brick and a clay tennis court. Groomed trails start right outside the front door with complimentary cross-country skis and snowshoe equipment. Or bring your books and find your own special place.

Check out the Windham Hill web site at www.windhamhill.com, the largest, most useful, most comprehensive we have seen to date.

Twenty-one rooms, each with private bath. $245–$370. Breakfast, dinner, and gratuity included. $50 additional during foliage season. Bed-and-breakfast rates $45 less per person.

Two-night weekend minimum. Children over 12 welcome. Third person in room $70 additional. No pets. No smoking. Dinner by advance reservation for outside diners $40. Located 1.2 miles off Route 30. RR1, Box 44, West Townshend, VT 05359; (802) 874-4080, (800) 944-4080; fax (802) 874-4702; www.windhamhill.com.

What to Do. Take a hike or go cross-country skiing on the inn's extensive private network of trails. You have a choice of downhill skiing close by at Stratton, Mount Snow, or Okemo. Drive the back roads of Vermont. Visit the tiny picture-book village of Grafton, which includes some of the finest existing examples of eighteenth-and nineteenth-century Vermont architecture. Stop by the Grafton Cheese Company and sample the award-winning Classic Reserve extrasharp cheddar, aged for two years. Take a drive to Woodstock, a preserved village with outstanding small shops and galleries. Its classic green is surrounded by examples of Georgian and Federal architecture. At the Billings Farm Museum you can trace the daily life of a Vermont family hill farm in 1890. Compare your stay at Windham Hill Inn, which was once a dairy farm, with the hard life of the families depicted at the Billings Museum. Continue to Quechee to see the glassblowers at the Simon Pearce glass mill. Shoppers flock to Manchester, less than an hour away, where there are more than seventy designer outlets and upscale boutiques including Cole-Haan, Burberry, Escada, Brooks Brothers, Coach, J. Crew, Ellen Tracy, T. S. E. Cashmere, Espirit, and Go Silk.

How to Get There. From Hartford, take I-91 north to Brattleboro. Take Route 30 north to West Townshend. Turn right at the sign in West Townshend for 1.2 miles to the inn.

Cornucopia of Dorset

Cornucopia of Dorset, *Dorset, Vermont*

You will be pampered to perfection at this intimate nineteenth-century white clapboard bed-and-breakfast located in the center of Dorset. After innkeeper Bill Ley showed us to our room, we went downstairs for a cup of tea and some cookies. Linda Ley offered us a flute of champagne, a glass of white wine, or a soft drink. Kitt, their well-trained purebred Vermont mutt, also welcomed us.

The entire first floor is common space for the guests. A glass-walled sitting area with a pair of white couches, a television, a VCR, picture books about Vermont, and a selection of current magazines occupies one end of the dining room. There is a small living room with a fireplace and a sitting area. The library has a backgammon table and easy chairs. The terrace is set with Adirondack chairs and overlooks the manicured, intensely cultivated narrow yard and the cottage.

The attention to detail is not limited to the decor. Bill or

Linda will make dinner reservations for you and then leave a written confirmation and a copy of the menu in your room. Before dinner they serve light hors d'oeuvres by candlelight and have a selection of champagne and wines available for purchase. After dinner we found our bed turned down, an oil lamp burning, a piece of Mother Myrick's buttercrunch candy or a Steininger's truffle on our pillows, and the morning breakfast menu. If you stay in the main house, you can have a pot of coffee or tea served in Royal Doulton china brought up to your room before breakfast.

All the rooms have down comforters in winter and colorful quilts in warmer months. Each room also has a notebook filled with information about the inn, the innkeepers, the local restaurants, the history of the area, and some things to do. The rooms are named after local mountains. We stayed in the Scallop, a corner room with floor-to-ceiling windows, a queen-size canopy bed, and a wood-burning fireplace. Dorset Hill, with a four-poster king-size bed, and Green Peak, a long, spacious room with a four-poster queen-size bed, both look out on the gardens; each has a gas fireplace. Mother Myrick, with a king-size bed, is the only room without a fireplace.

For a romantic getaway, stay in Owl's Head, a private cottage located behind the inn. The first-floor living room has a cathedral ceiling, wide-board pine floors, a couch, and an easy chair facing a brick fireplace. A full kitchen, an outdoor deck with chairs, and the bath also are on the first floor. From the sleeping loft, which has a queen-size bed and two skylights, you can look down into the living room.

The Cornucopia's large breakfast room has an exquisite eighteen-by-twenty-five-foot-Oriental rug and French doors that open onto the terrace and gardens. Breakfast includes freshly squeezed juice, a fruit salad, and an entrée such as a baked puff pancake served with fresh fruit and warm maple syrup, rum raisin French toast, or croissant à l'orange. At breakfast we were entertained by a flock of evening grosbeaks gathered at the window bird feeders.

Four rooms and one cottage suite, each with private bath. Rooms, $115–$175; cottage, $200–$245. Inquire about seasonal specials such as dinner for two, theater, or alpine skiing tickets. Full breakfast and hors d'oeuvres included. Children over 16 welcome. Rooms are double occupancy only. No pets. No smoking. Two-night weekend minimum. Route 30, Dorset, VT 05251; (802) 867-5751, (800) 566-5751; fax (802) 867-5753; www.CORNUCOPIAofDORSET.com.

Where to Dine.   Walk next door to Barrows House (802) 867-4455) and try the Maine crab cakes, a house specialty prepared with Old Bay seasoning, or salmon stuffed with sun-dried tomatoes, pine nuts, basil, and cream cheese.

Go over Dorset Hill to East Dorset and have an elegant dinner at Chantecleer (Route 7A; (802) 362-1616), the best restaurant in this area. Try an appetizer of risotto with mushrooms and sausage, a Caesar salad prepared tableside, or potato pancakes served with a thick crabmeat-and-lime-butter sauce. The cheese fondue makes a fun meal, and the rack of lamb is carved tableside.

The tavern at the venerable old Dorset Inn (Route 30; (802) 867-5500) is one of the gathering spots and watering holes favored by the locals. Drive about 15 miles southwest to Steininger's, in Salem, New York, for lunch (Main Street; (518) 854-3830). Try a bowl of the homemade soup and a cup of cappuccino. The chocolates are made in the finest European tradition.

What to Do.   Walk around Dorset, an idyllic Vermont village. The buildings are white with black or dark green shutters. Peltier's General Store was built in 1817. A few miles down the road is Williams Department Store, an old-fashioned "no frills" store that's been owned by the same family for 100 years. Notice the marble sidewalks and the marble church. Dorset is the site of the first marble quarry on the North American continent. The stone for the New York Public Library came from one of the local quarries, which now is a favorite swimming hole.

Route 30 going north out of Dorset runs through the Mettowee Valley for 17 miles. This is picture-perfect rural Vermont scenery—a valley of dairy and sheep farms, farmhouses, silos, and tillable land. Visit Hildene, the home of Robert Todd Lincoln. Go canoeing or fishing on the Battenkill River, hike on the Appalachian Trail, or play golf on the newly built Glen Eagles course at the Equinox Hotel. Shoppers will want to head to the designer discount stores in Manchester: Anne Klein, Cole-Haan, Polo/Ralph Lauren, Donna Karan, Hickey Freeman, Coach Leatherware, Joan and David, Brooks Brothers, and many more.

How to Get There.   From New York City, take the New York Thruway (I-87) to I-787 to Troy. Head east on New York State Route 7 (which becomes Route 9 in Vermont) to Bennington. Take U.S. Route 7 north to Manchester and Route 30 to Dorset. From Hartford, take I-91 north to Brattleboro, then Route 30 west to Manchester Center. Continue 6 miles to Dorset. From Boston, take the Massachusetts Turnpike (I-90) west to I-91 north, then follow the directions above.

Love Letters Room at The Village Country Inn

The Village Country Inn, *Manchester Village, Vermont*

The Village Country Inn is ideally situated in historic Manchester Village. For the shopper, one need go less than a mile down the road to take advantage of the vast numbers of upscale outlets; for those who like to stroll, Manchester Village has marble sidewalks, historic homes, and galleries; and for those who like to relax at the inn, the chintz-pillowed rockers on the front porch, the chaises around the large pool, or benches in the garden are most inviting.

Since purchasing this 100-year-old building in 1985, innkeepers Anne and Jay Degen have done major renovations. They tore down walls to create large rooms and suites that Anne, who has outstanding interior decorating skills, has elegantly transformed with bolts and bolts of lace, plush car-pets, and flowered fabrics and wallpaper to create a French country romantic feel. "Renoir and Monet are my favorite art-ists," Anne told us as she proudly showed us the flower gar-den with a half-moon bridge and fountains that create the same feel in flowers as inside the inn.

Room choices include two-room suites or large luxury rooms, garden rooms with private entrances, and smaller standard accommodations called sleeping rooms. All the rooms have phones, and the larger accommodations have televisions. For a romantic stay pick one of the newly reno-vated large luxury rooms or suites. Le Fleur and Rose Noir each have a king-size bed and overlook the garden. Le Fleur has a separate sitting room with white wicker furniture and a large bath with a clawfoot tub on a platform and a separate shower. Rose Noir is an oversize room with a complete sitting area with a wet bar and a gas fireplace, a large bath with a soaking tub for two on a raised platform, and a separate shower. The Janées Suite has a more formal feel with an es-pecially large living room with a gas fireplace, a separate bed-room with a queen-size bed, and a new bath. Francesca's Room is an oversize room with a king-size canopy bed, a large bath with a clawfoot tub on a pedestal, a shower with a curved glass door, and a separate toilet room. Renaissance is the same size room but has a queen-size bed with carved head-board and footboard and a new bath. Lavender and Lace has a king-size canopy bed decorated with ivy, and Love Letters has a queen-size canopy bed draped with ecru lace.

The two newest luxury rooms are Chantels Boudoir and Victoria's Room. Chantels Boudoir has a ceiling-mount bed canopy, a sitting area with a gas fireplace, and a large bath. Victoria's Room has a queen-size bed, a gas fireplace, and a large bath with a double whirlpool tub and a separate shower.

The four garden rooms are popular, particularly in the summer, as you can open your door and walk directly into the garden. Apricot Meadow and the Country Garden Room each have king-size canopy beds, and their doors face the garden. Victorian Rose, the largest of the garden rooms, with a king-size canopy bed, and Tea Rose, with a queen-size canopy bed, have private entrances on the side of the inn and overlook the heart garden. The lower-priced sleeping rooms are smaller in size, perfectly adequate if you don't want to spend a lot of time in your room, and offer one of the best values in Manchester Village. The lowest priced rooms have double beds, and those that are larger have queen-size beds. None of the standard rooms have televisions.

For a romantic getaway the inn offers a couple of packages. The most popular, the Enchanted Evening, includes a series of cards with things to do within the inn, dinner in the dining room, followed by a surprise when the couple return to their room. A midweek package includes a candlelit dinner served in one of the suites. And during the summer you can arrange for a romantic lunch in the new white Victorian gazebo in the garden.

Since the Degens have added the new garden and fountains, the outdoor marble terrace next to the pool is an inviting summer dining option. The candlelit dining room has a French country feel with hunter and ecru flowered wallpaper and white trellises with ivy. Dinner includes choices of appetizer, salad, and entrée, and a selection from the dessert tray.

For starters we suggest escargot Bourguignonne or the smoked seafood. Eight entrée selections are offered nightly, including a vegetarian dish and a lighter-fare option such as sautéed chicken with rosemary in a light broth served with white rice and a steamed vegetable. A favorite is the rack of lamb with mint pesto, sautéed veal medallions with a merlot demi glaze, and the fresh seafood selection of the day.

Thirty-three rooms and suites, each with private bath. Standard rooms, $150–$185; garden rooms and suites, $195–$350. Full breakfast and dinner for two included. 15% service charge. Not appropriate for children. No smoking. No pets. Located on Historic Route 7A. Box 408, Manchester Village, VT 05254; (802) 362-1792, (800) 370-0300; fax (802) 362-7238; www.villagecountryinn.com.

What to Do. Shoppers flock to Manchester and its more than seventy designer outlets and upscale boutiques, including Ralph Lauren, Armani, Ellen Tracy, and Brooks Brothers. Visit Hildene, the home of Robert Todd Lincoln; go canoeing on the Battenkill River; go golfing at Glen Eagles or the Manchester Country Club; and visit antiques shops and galleries. The best downhill skiing in the area is at Stratton.

How to Get There. From New York City, take the New York Thruway (I-87) to I-787 to Troy. Head east on Route 7 to Route 9 to Bennington. Take Route 7 to Manchester, then go south on Route 7A to the inn. From Hartford, take I-91 north to Brattleboro; go west on Route 30 to Manchester and south on Route 7A to the inn. From Boston, take the Massachusetts Turnpike (I-90) west to I-91 north to Brattleboro. Then follow the directions above.

© Dave Kutchukian

The Reluctant Panther

The Reluctant Panther, *Manchester Village, Vermont*

The distinctive color of the main building, mauve with yellow shutters, makes this inn, located in the center of Manchester Village next to the Equinox Hotel, stand out. Unlike many other innkeepers, Robert Bachofen was trained in hotel management in Switzerland. Before purchasing the inn Robert had a top position at the Plaza Hotel in New York City. Maye, his wife, also had a career in hotel management.

The Mary Porter House, an adjacent building, has large deluxe rooms and suites. The handicap-accessible 700-square-foot Garden Suite has a bedroom with a massive king-size mahogany bed, a terra-cotta floor with area rugs, and a see-through gas fireplace that is visible from the bed as well as from the bath, which has a double whirlpool tub and a separate shower. The suite includes a sitting room with a second gas fireplace, and a private porch. The Mark Skinner Suite is a top favorite for purists who like wood-burning fireplaces; the bedroom has a king-size brass bed facing a wood-burning fireplace, a porch, and an enormous bathroom with a double whirlpool in the center of the room, a separate shower, double pedestal sinks, and another wood-burning fireplace. The Seminary Suite is especially spacious. It has a king-size bed, a wood-burning fireplace with a sitting area including a couch and an easy chair, windows on three sides, and a large bath with a double whirlpool tub. The Mary Porter Room has a king-size four-poster bed and two fireplaces, one in the bedroom and another in the bathroom, which also has a double whirlpool tub. The Village Suite has a bedroom with a king-size bed and a woodstove, a separate sitting area with a convertible couch, and a bath with two distinctive turquoise pedestal sinks, a marble-tiled floor, and a whirlpool.

The conference room is being converted into the Pond View Suite, which will be the most luxurious at the inn. It will be approximately 850 square feet and will have two large fireplaces, a double whirlpool tub, a cathedral ceiling, French windows along one side of the room, and a large private terrace.

In the main inn, Room J, a deluxe room with a king-size bed, Pierre Deux fabrics, a wood-burning fireplace, and windows on three sides, is one of the larger rooms frequently selected by honeymooners. Room B, a deluxe, very inviting wood-burning fireplace room, is also a favorite, it has a king-size bed, easy chairs near the fireplace, and the best view of Mount Equinox. Rooms C and F are junior suites with king-size beds and wood-burning fireplaces. Room M is a new room with a gas fireplace in the bedroom, a bath with an oversize marble shower, and a separate living room.

For a romantic getaway on a budget stay in one of the smaller standard rooms, which do not have fireplaces. Room A, a favorite, is small but bright with windows on two sides and a bed that can be made up as twins or one king-size bed. Other lower-priced choices are Room C, with a queen-size bed, and Room E, with a king-size bed. All of the rooms have telephones, televisions, custom-made shades that coordinate with the window treatments, and matching goose down comforters.

Breakfast is elegantly served at individual marble-topped tables from 8:30 to 9:30 A.M. The day we stayed we had juice, a fruit plate, French toast, and bacon. Large corn or blueberry muffins are always served.

Guests have access to the sports facilities (for a fee) at the Equinox Hotel. There is also a fine conference room in a separate building that includes a large television, a VCR, and comfortable executive seating for twenty-five.

Before dinner sit in the bar or on the outside terrace to have a drink before moving to the intimate dining room with greenhouse window. Robert is the chef. The menu features a number of dishes from Switzerland. For starters get raclette, a Swiss dish of melted cheese (it is melted in the kitchen, not at the table) served with boiled potatoes and pickles. Spanakopita, a phyllo dough filled with spinach and chèvre, carpaccio of beef with grated horseradish, and cream of curried carrot soup are other appetizers. Included among the dozen or more entrées are Wiener schnitzel with rosemary spaetzle, roasted pair of quail with a peppercorn sauce, grilled New York strip steak with a mustard seed crust, braised lamb shank with garlic-Parmesan polenta, baked salmon in a potato crust, and Swiss veal sautéed with mushrooms.

Seventeen rooms and suites, each with private bath. $138–$288. Breakfast and dinner for two included. 15% service charge. Foliage season, Christmas week, and holiday weekends, $195–$335. Bed-and-breakfast rates (when the restaurant is closed), deduct $40. No pets. Children over 14

welcome. Third person in room $65. Dinner served week-
ends; entrées $17–$27. Three-course prix fixe $36. West
Road and Route 7A. Box 678, Manchester Village, VT 05254;
(802) 362-2568, (800) 822-2331; fax (802) 362-2586; www.
reluctantpanther.com.

Where to Dine. The Reluctant Panther features Swiss
specialties. The best restaurant in the area is Chantecleer,
which serves traditional French food in a converted barn with
a magnificent fieldstone fireplace (Route 7A, East Dorset;
(802) 362-1616). The Equinox Hotel (802) 362-4700) is next
door. Other good choices are Mistral's for fine dining (Toll
Gate Road, just outside Manchester on Route 30; (802) 362-
1779) with a great view of a rushing stream. Bistro Henry is
good for more casual fare (Routes 11 and 30; (802) 362-4982).
If you like northern Italian cooking, try Vittorio's (1 Prospect
Street; (802) 442-3210), an out-of-the-way storefront restaurant
in North Bennington.

What to Do. Shoppers flock to Manchester and its more
than seventy designer outlets and upscale boutiques, including Orvis, Anne Klein, Ralph Lauren, Coach, Harvé Bernard,
Liz Claiborne, Hickey Freeman, Ellen Tracy, and Brooks
Brothers. Visit Hildene, the home of Robert Todd Lincoln;
attend the Orvis fly-fishing or shooting school; go canoeing
on the Battenkill River; golf on the new Glen Eagles course
at the Equinox; drive over the Green Mountains on the Kelly
Stand Road; see a performance at the Dorset or Weston Playhouse; and visit the antiques shops and galleries in the area.
The best downhill ski area is at Stratton.

How to Get There. From New York City, take the New
York Thruway (I-87) to 1-787 to Troy. Head east on Route 7

and then take Route 9 to Bennington. Take Route 7 to Manchester, then head south on Route 7A, 1 mile to the inn. From Hartford, take I-91 to Brattleboro, go west on Route 9 to Bennington, then north on Route 7 to Manchester.

1811 House

1811 House, *Manchester Village, Vermont*

An inn is far more than the sum of its details. You'll know that this inn is in a class by itself as soon as you walk through the door. The original structure was built in the 1770s and has been operated as an inn since 1811. The Victorian porches that were added later have been taken away, excessive molding recently was removed, and modern windowpanes were replaced with old handmade glass. Today the house is a showcase for an extensive collection of English and American antiques, prints, and Oriental rugs that the previous owners accumulated. Innkeepers Marnie and Bruce Duff purchased the inn along with almost all of the furnishings in July 1990. Since then they have greatly expanded the perennial gardens and have fully air-conditioned the buildings.

In the wood-paneled foyer there is a woodcut of the current 1811 House. Beyond is a little English pub called a "snug." High chairs are placed around the polished wood bar; the dark wood tables by the windows are rubbed to a shine; and a fireplace, Windsor chairs, and a regulation dart board add to the cozy atmosphere. Marnie and Bruce have put their Scottish coat of arms above the bar. The glasses are Waterford, and the liquor selection includes Bruce's collection of forty-three single-malt scotch whiskeys. When the inn isn't busy, the bar operates on the honor system. Most evenings it's open to the public for a few hours.

One feature of the 1811 House that we found particularly appealing was the variety of common rooms available to guests. A library and a living room each have a working fireplace. The common rooms have literature about area attractions and decanters of sherry and port set out for guests. A basement game room is given atmosphere with low overhead lamps and has both table tennis and a regulation billiards table. The formal dining room, with another fireplace and three separate tables, is a great place for a bridge tournament.

The most romantic rooms are the six with fireplaces and the one with a private balcony. Three of these are located in a newly reconstructed cottage next to the main inn. Our favorite cottage room takes up the entire second floor and has a peaked ceiling. The fireplace is in full view of the king-size bed and the two enormous leather chairs. On the first floor are two additional rooms, each with a king-size canopy bed, easy chairs, an Oriental rug, and a large modern bath.

In the main inn, the fireplace rooms include the suite on the first floor, with a king-size four-poster, and the two rooms on the second floor, each with a queen-size canopy bed. All the rooms have Oriental rugs and reading chairs. The baths in the main inn are not as large as those in the cottage, although they have old-fashioned clawfoot tubs. If you are visiting during the warmer months ask for the Robinson Room; its king-size bed faces glass doors that open onto a private balcony. The balcony view of the landscaped grounds, pond, and Green Mountains is positively breathtaking. The marble enclosure around the clawfoot tub also lends an air of individuality to this room.

A full breakfast is served from 8 to 9:30 A.M. The choice is yours whether to have it in the snug or in the more formal dining room. Breakfast includes fresh orange or grapefruit juice, fresh fruit, and a different entrée each day. On Saturday it's an English-style breakfast of fried eggs, scones, bacon, grilled tomatoes, apples, and mushrooms. On Sundays it's eggs Benedict. Other days it might be omelettes with fried potatoes and English muffins, or pancakes with maple syrup.

Thirteen rooms and one suite, each with private bath. $120–$220. Full breakfast included. Children over 16 welcome. No pets. Two-night minimum on weekends and during the fall foliage season. Box 39, Route 7A, Manchester Village, VT 05254; (802) 362-1811, (800) 432-1811; fax (802) 362-2443.

Where to Dine.   The best restaurant in the area is Chantecleer, which serves traditional French food in a converted barn with a magnificent fieldstone fireplace (Route 7A, East Dorset; (802) 362-1616). The Equinox Hotel (802) 362-4700) and the Reluctant Panther (802) 362-2568) are across the street from the 1811 House. Other good choices are Mistral's for fine dining (Toll Gate Road, just outside Manchester on Route 30; (802) 362-1779) and Bistro Henry for more casual fare (Routes 11 and 30, Manchester; (802) 362-4982).

What to Do. Shoppers flock to Manchester and its more than seventy designer outlets and upscale boutiques, including Orvis, Anne Klein, Ralph Lauren, Coach, Harvé Bernard, Liz Claiborne, Hickey Freeman, Ellen Tracy, and Brooks Brothers. Visit Hildene, the home of Robert Todd Lincoln; attend the Orvis fly-fishing or shooting school; canoe on the Battenkill River or golf on the new Glen Eagles course at the Equinox; and drive over the Green Mountains on the Kelly Stand Road. See a performance at the Dorset or Weston Playhouse and visit the antiques shops and galleries in the area. The two closest ski areas are Bromley and Stratton. For cross-country skiing, try Stratton, Hildene, or Wild Wing.

How to Get There. From New York City, take the New York State Thruway (1-87) north to I-787 to Troy. Head east on New York State Route 7, which becomes Route 9 east at the Vermont–New York border. Continue east on Route 9 to Bennington. Take U.S. Route 7 north to Manchester, then go south on Route 7A, 1 mile to the inn. From Hartford, take I-91 north to Brattleboro. Go west on Route 30 to Manchester. Go south on Route 7A, 1 mile to the inn. From Boston, take the Massachusetts Turnpike (I-90) west to I-91 north. Then follow the directions above.

Doug Mindell

The Inn at Ormsby Hill

The Inn at Ormsby Hill, *Manchester Center, Vermont*

This large Federal manor house located about a mile south of Manchester Village had its origins in the 1760s. Robert Todd Lincoln (son of Abraham Lincoln) and President Howard Taft stayed here.

Innkeepers Ted and Chris Sprague, who formerly owned an inn on the Maine coast, have done major renovations to this property. With the combination of a panoramic view of the Green Mountains, spacious common areas, renovated and new rooms (nine with wood-burning or gas fireplaces and double whirlpool tubs), and a creative gourmet breakfast, this inn is now one of the best in this area. The interior has an open feel with three large common areas for guests. We like the more casual gathering room, with the original oversize wood-burning fireplace, and the conservatory, a very large room with a dining room table, a fireplace, and seating by the wraparound glass windows facing the Green Mountains.

The Tower, a suite on three levels, is the most private accommodation and has a second-floor bedroom with a gas fireplace and a queen-size canopy bed. The bath is up a winding staircase (on the third floor) and has a double whirlpool tub, a steam shower, and eight windows with excellent views of the hillside.

The Taft Room is the second most popular room as it has a very large bedroom. It has a king-size canopy bed, a vaulted ceiling, and a wood-burning fireplace, plus a large bath with the largest double whirlpool in the inn and a separate two-person shower. The Pierrepont Room and Anne Eliza, newly built rooms, have antique king-size bow canopy beds and gas fireplaces that you can see from the beds as well as from the whirlpool tubs. The Library, a first-floor handicap-accessible room, has the original hand-hewn beam ceiling, a queen-size canopy bed, a wood-burning fireplace, and a bath with double whirlpool tub and separate two-person shower. Ethan Allen, a quiet room with a private outdoor entrance, has a queen-size canopy bed, a gas fireplace, and a double whirlpool tub from which you can see the fireplace as well as get a view of the mountains. Lincoln, a very spacious room, has a four-poster king-size bed, a thermostatically controlled gas fireplace, and a double whirlpool tub. All the rooms are air-conditioned. Other nice touches are terry-cloth lined robes, a plate of cookies in your room, and turndown service.

A creative gourmet breakfast buffet is available from 8 to 10 A.M. with the hot entrée served at 9, followed by dessert. We were served blueberry-peach crisp, strawberry frappé, and a memorable dish of creamy risotto with pancetta and grilled sliced portabello mushrooms. Other popular main dishes include roasted garlic portabello mushrooms topped with basil-and-tomato scrambled eggs, or baked orange French toast. Breakfast desserts are gingerbread, cobblers, or fruit tarts served with vanilla ice cream.

On Friday nights Chris prepares an informal dinner such as baked pasta with shiitake mushrooms and tomatoes, linguine with shrimp and vegetables, or ziti casserole with turkey meatballs; homemade bread; and dessert, available from 6:30 to 9 P.M. On Saturday night Chris prepares a single four-course gourmet dinner, with hors d'oeuvres served at 6:30 P.M. and dinner served at 7 P.M. It includes an appetizer such as arugula and porcini risotto; leek, bacon, and Stilton polenta with tomato sauce; or tomato, basil, and phyllo tart. A mesclun salad follows. The entrée might be rack of lamb with shiitake mushrooms, roast salmon on a celery root purée, or tenderloin of pork with port and dried cranberries, followed by dessert of warm puff pastry with pastry cream, raspberries, and caramel sauce or triple chocolate torte with white chocolate sauce.

Ten rooms, each with private bath. $160–$240. $50 additional during foliage season and for some holidays. Afternoon tea and breakfast included. Not appropriate for young children. No smoking. No pets. Friday supper, $20 for two; Saturday dinner, $65 for two. Two night weekend minimum. On Historic Route 7A. RR2, Box 3264, Manchester Center, VT 05255; (802) 362-1163, (800) 670-2841; fax (800) 362-5176; www.ormsbyhill.com.

Where to Dine.   If you like northern Italian cooking try Vittorio's (1 Prospect Street, North Bennington; (802) 442-3210), an out-of-the-way storefront restaurant. Chantecleer serves traditional French food in a converted barn with a magnificent fieldstone fireplace (Route 7A, East Dorset; (802) 362-1616). The Equinox Hotel (Route 7A, Manchester Village; (802) 362-4700) and the Reluctant Panther (Route 7A, Manchester Village; (802) 362-2568) are just up the road. Other good choices are Mistral's (Toll Gate Road (Route 30), Manchester; (802) 362-1779) for fine dining and Bistro Henry (Routes 11 and 30, Manchester; (802) 362-4982) for more casual fare.

What to Do.   Shoppers flock to Manchester and its more than seventy designer outlets and upscale boutiques including Orvis, Anne Klein, Ralph Lauren, Coach, Tommy Hilfiger, Liz Claiborne, Hickey Freeman, Ellen Tracy, and Brooks Brothers. Visit Hildene, the home of Robert Todd Lincoln; canoe on the Battenkill River or golf on the new Glen Eagles course at the Equinox; and drive over the Green Mountains on the Kelly Stand Road. See a performance at the Dorset or Weston Playhouse and visit the antiques shops and galleries in the area. The two closest ski areas are Bromley and Stratton. For cross-country skiing, try Hildene or Wild Wings.

How to Get There.   From New York City, take the New York State Thruway (I-87) north to exit 23, then I-787 north to Route 7 east, which becomes Route 9 east at the New York–Vermont border. In Bennington, take Route 7 north. Take exit 3, turn left on Route 313, then go right on Historic Route 7A. The inn is 8 miles on the right. From Hartford, take I-91 north to Brattleboro. Go west on Route 30 to Manchester. Go south on Route 7A for 3 miles. From Boston, take the Massachusetts Turnpike (I-90) west to I-91 north. Then follow the directions above.

Cliffwood Inn

Cliffwood Inn, *Lenox, Massachusetts*

Set back from the road on one and a half acres on a quiet street of large, elegant homes, two blocks from the center of Lenox, stands Cliffwood Inn. This 1889 mansion, built during the Belle Epoque period for Edward Livingston, a diplomat to France, is in the grand Stanford White style. The circular drive leads to an impressive portico supported by eight Ionic columns and a heavy carved wooden door framed by decorative mullioned windows.

Outfitting an inn with fine furnishings was no problem for owners Joy and Scottie Farrelly, as they had amassed a sizable collection of furniture, paintings, Oriental rugs, and accessories during seventeen years of corporate moves among the capitals of Europe. Over the years they commissioned furniture makers in France, Italy, and Belgium to craft reproductions of museum pieces that would complement the antiques they purchased. They even had an artist copy several of Canaletto's Venetian scenes. The Farrellys are also dealers in Eldred Wheeler Colonial reproduction furniture and use over thirty pieces in furnishing the rooms.

Polished inlaid hardwood floors, twelve-foot ceilings, and four working wood-burning fireplaces distinguish the first floor. In keeping with the magnitude of the house, there's a grand piano in the front hall. Huge gilded mirrors make the expansive living room, comfortably arranged with sofas and easy chairs, appear extraordinarily large.

In the summer, breakfast is served on the 850-square-foot veranda, which overlooks the pool and landscaped grounds. The dining room is graced by a Venetian chandelier and a 400-year-old sideboard. Except for midweek during the off-season, there is a copious continental breakfast with fresh fruit, hot fruit compote, or baked apples with crème fraiche; homemade granola; juice; popovers and muffins, or Belgian waffles. The Farrellys use their new English AGA Cooker (a cast-iron stove with four ovens) to cook baked eggs, bacon, and turkey breakfast sausages.

The second-floor sitting area includes a large bookcase filled with art books neatly arranged by country of origin. A major advantage for guests at Cliffwood is Scottie Farrelly's computerized listing of performances by the more than forty different arts groups that call the Berkshires home during the summer months. When you make your reservation, be sure to ask for a listing of events coinciding with your stay.

Six of the seven bedrooms, which are named for ancestors of the Farrellys, have wood-burning fireplaces. The Helen Walker Room, one of the largest, has a king-size four-poster canopy bed, a chaise longue, a fireplace, and a newly reno-vated bathroom with a whirlpool tub. We were quite taken with the Jacob Gross Jr. Room, which has a king-size canopy bed, a writing desk, easy chairs, a fireplace, and a private balcony. The bath includes a bidet. The Walker/Linton Suite includes a bedroom with a queen-size four-poster canopy bed and a sitting room with a convertible couch and a fireplace. The Nathaniel Foote Room, on the third floor, is an especially comfortable large room with two wingback chairs in front of the fireplace, a queen-size four-poster canopy bed, and Oriental rugs.

A unique feature is the new indoor countercurrent pool, a small pool with an adjustable current, and there is a whirlpool large enough for three or four people.

The location of the inn makes it ideally suited for music lovers; not only is Cliffwood in Lenox, but the street the inn is on leads directly to an entrance to Tanglewood that bypasses the usual traffic jams. In addition, the landscaped grounds, the large swimming pool, and the many restaurants and shops nearby make this a getaway where a car is not an absolute necessity. Visitors from abroad might be pleased to know that Joy and Scottie Farrelly speak French, Italian, and Spanish.

Seven rooms, each with private bath. July, August, and foliage season, weekends, $132–$231; other times, $87–$155. Continental breakfast (except midweek in low season) and wine and hors d'oeuvres included. Three-or four-night weekend minimum in high season. Children over 11 welcome. Third person $35 additional. No pets. No smoking. 25 Cliffwood Street, Lenox, MA 01240; (413) 637-3330, (800) 789-3331; fax (413) 637-0221; www.cliffwood.com.

Where to Dine.   For the ultimate in palatial surroundings and preparation, head to Wheatleigh (West Hawthorne Road; (413) 637-0610), in Lenox. Cranwell (413) 637-1364, year-round) and Blantyre (413) 637-3556, summer and fall) are two other mansions with elegant restaurants (both are off Route 20 in Lenox). The Village Inn (413) 637-0020, Church Street Café (413) 637-2745), and Café Lucia (413) 637-2640) are all on Church Street and are within walking distance of the inn. Other good choices are La Tomate, in Great Barrington, and La Bruschetta (413) 232-7141), in West Stockbridge.

What to Do.   For more than fifty years, the Boston Symphony Orchestra has been instrumental in turning the Berkshire region into one of the great summer cultural destinations in the country. The orchestra performs during July and August at Tanglewood. Performances by over forty area art groups are all available nearby—such as Berkshire Theatre Festival, Jacob's Pillow Dance Festival, Shakespeare & Company, Edith Wharton Play Matinees, and the Williamstown Theatre Festival, in nearby Williamstown. The new Norman Rockwell Museum, which houses more than 600 of the artist's paintings and drawings, is located 2 miles from Stockbridge.

Herman Melville wrote the great American novel *Moby Dick* at Arrowhead, his home, located outside Pittsfield. The Clark Art Institute, in Williamstown, has an outstanding collection of seventeenth-through-nineteenth-century paintings, including works by Gainsborough, Rembrandt, Renoir, Degas, Monet, Cassatt, and Remington. The Hancock Shaker Village, near Pittsfield, is an outstanding museum comprised of twenty buildings where you watch craftspeople weave baskets and make brooms, chairs, and oval Shaker boxes.

How to Get There.   From New York City, take the Taconic State Parkway north to the Massachusetts Turnpike (I-90) east. From the Lee exit, take Route 20 to Route 7A north to Lenox. From Boston, take the Massachusetts Turnpike to the Lee exit and follow the directions above.

Wheatleigh

Wheatleigh, *Lenox, Massachusetts*

This Florentine-inspired palace built in 1893, a romantic elegant small country hotel on twenty-two acres, is close to the back entrance of Tanglewood. The palace has an airy uncluttered contemporary feel. The Great Hall has a baronial marble wood-burning fireplace, a grand piano, large plants, and Linfield and Susan Simon's (the Simons are the owners) museum-quality collection of ceramics attractively offset by English antiques and Orientals. The sweeping staircase and the captivating views of the Berkshire Hills from the glass doors leading to the terrace add to the magnificence of the setting. The Great Hall and the guest rooms were redecorated in 1993.

Here we found spacious accommodations, lots of privacy, and a dining experience second to none. The top choices are the five very large rooms on the second floor that overlook the hills and 1C, on the first floor, which looks out on the gardens. Each of these rooms has a king-size bed and a fireplace. Five of these rooms also have balconies. The center room, the former sitting room between the Count's Room and the Countess's Room, is the most interesting architecturally as it has a dome ceiling and curved walls, but it has a small bath.

Superior rooms are slightly smaller but are still of good size. They generally overlook the front or the side so they don't have sweeping long views; three of these rooms also have fireplaces. The Aviary, a most unusual accommodation with a more rustic feel, is a duplex. The first floor has two queen-size beds with a narrow spiral staircase leading to the second floor, with two twin beds and a bath.

The best of the lower-priced choices (small rooms, approximately eleven by thirteen feet) is a first-floor room (ID) with a high ceiling, a queen-size bed, and French doors opening onto the portico (a particularly good choice in the summer). The grounds include an oval-shaped swimming pool set in a grove of towering pines, a tennis court, a small fitness room, and a massage room.

The entrance to the formal dining room is through the Great Hall. A pair of antique Waterford chandeliers, two matching candelabra above the fireplace, and candlelit tables set the stage. The dining here is on the cutting edge of culinary innovation. Three five-course tasting menus are prepared each evening—a low fat, a vegetarian, and a dinner menu. We had a truly memorable dinner, choosing courses from each of the three menus. The low-fat dinner the night we dined included seviche of scallops, pumpkin soup with fresh fig quenelles, grilled steelhead salmon with Provençale vegetables, breast of squab, a trio of sorbets, and a poached spiced seckel pear.

The vegetarian menu included three vegetable mousses

with a gazpacho sauce, Monterey chèvre and roasted vegetable terrine, wild mushroom Napoleon, acorn squash filled with wild rice and pecans, fresh mission figs in red wine sauce with frozen anisette soufflé, and white and dark chocolate mousse with raspberries in a delicate pastry. The dinner tasting menu included smoked salmon on buckwheat blini with ossetra caviar, foie gras terrine wrapped in thin slices of potato, halibut with a black trumpet mushroom sauce, roast veal with black truffle sauce and a wild mushroom ravioli, a selection of cheeses, and a tarte tatin with sour cream quenelles. Each dish was beautifully coordinated with the china on which it was served. The portions are small and light, so we left the table full but not as stuffed as one would expect after this number of courses. The wine list is extensive and expensive; all the great French growths are represented. A second dining option during the summer is the Grill Room. In nice weather, dining on the portico takes advantage of the mountain views. Selections include Thai-style free-range chicken, bouillabaisse, grilled salmon or swordfish, and smoked turkey sandwich.

Seventeen rooms, each with private bath. July, August, and fall weekends, $255–$625; other times, $175–$475. 9% service charge. Breakfast is available but is not included. Children over 9 are welcome. Third person $25 additional. No pets. July and August, lunch and dinner daily. Other times of the year, dinner on weekends and some midweek nights. Prix fixe tasting dinners and pretheater dinner in the summer, $75; dégustation dinner, $90. Grill Room: Sunday brunch and dinner, July and August, entrées, $17–$24; lunch entrées, $12–$20. Hawthorne Road (off Route 183), Lenox, MA 01240; (413) 637-0610; fax (413) 637-4507; www.wheatleigh.com.

What to Do.   The Berkshires are the home of fifty different organizations that offer music, dance, theater, film and art exhibits during the summer months—and increasingly throughout the year. For concerts go to Tanglewood in Lenox; for dance go to Jacob's Pillow in Beckett; for theater go to Williamstown or to the Berkshire Theatre Festival in Stockbridge. The top museums in the area are the Clark Art Institute, the Norman Rockwell Museum, the Hancock Shaker Village, and Chesterwood.

How to Get There. From Boston, take the Massachusetts Turnpike (I-90) west to the Lee exit. Go north on Route 20 to Route 7A into Lenox. In Lenox, go west on Route 183, then left onto West Hawthorne Street (just beyond Tanglewood). From New York City, take the Taconic State Parkway north to the Massachusetts Turnpike, then go east to the Lee exit and follow the directions above.

Lincoln Russell

Blantyre

The Blantyre, *Lenox, Massachusetts*

A long drive winds through the woods of this eighty-five acre property to the impressively maintained 1902 Tudor castle, which was patterned after one in Scotland. Staying here gives you a rare chance to experience what life was like for the very well-to-do at the turn of the century. Now this castle is owned by the Fitzpatricks, owners of the Red Lion and Country Curtains, and for many years it has been most capably managed by Roderick Anderson.

The Great Hall has dark carved wood paneling, a large wood-burning fireplace, Oriental rugs, and an array of upscale magazines spread on the large library table. The Music Room has a harp, a Steinway piano, a Tiffany lamp, and French crystal chandeliers. The first floor includes a main dining room and smaller side rooms used for dinner as well as a conservatory and an outdoor terrace where lunch is served in the summer.

To get the feel for living in the gilded age stay in the main house, which has five large rooms and suites, each with a wood-burning fireplace, and three modest-size rooms. The Paterson Suite is the pièce de résistance, with a huge bedroom with a king-size bed, a sitting room with a fireplace, and two bathrooms. The Cranwell and Laurel Suites are similar, each has a dressing room, a bedroom with a queen-size bed, and a wood-burning fireplace. For a summer stay we prefer the Cranwell, as it has a private balcony. The Blue Room, with two double beds, and the Corner Room, with a queen-size bed, each have a wood-burning fireplace.

The Carriage House provides a more casual setting, with a landscaped private patio off each room and marble baths. There are two suites, each with a sitting room, a bedroom with a queen-size canopy bed, and two marble baths. The three loft suites each have a living room, a deck, and a marble bath on the entry level, with an iron spiral staircase leading to a sleeping loft with a queen-size bed. Seven additional rooms in this building include two with king-size beds, four with queen-size beds (two have canopies), and one with two double beds.

In addition, three cottages on the property are now available. Winter Palace has a kitchenette, a large bedroom with a king-size bed, and a newly redone living room with a wood-stove and a veranda. Cottage by the Path has two bedrooms, one with a queen-size bed and one with twins, a living room with a wood-burning fireplace, a kitchen, and a patio. Cottage Queen, a handicap-accessible suite, has a king-size bed, a double-sided wood-burning fireplace visible from the bedroom and the sitting room, a bath with a tub and a separate shower, and a veranda.

A fruit-and-cheese plate greets each guest upon arrival. All rooms have phones, televisions, and central air-conditioning. Breakfast can be served to you in the main dining room or in your room.

During the Tanglewood season it is difficult to get reservations—in addition to being an elegant, deluxe hideaway, Tanglewood guest artists often stay here. Therefore, room requests are taken but are not confirmed until January, when the artists' schedules are finalized.

Dinner at Blantyre is in the grand tradition of an English country house. Guests are greeted in the Gothic Great Hall, with its massive furniture, leaded-glass windows, fireplace, tapestries, and Orientals. Have a drink and canapés here and make your dinner selections before being seated in the main dining room or in one of the smaller side rooms at widely spaced tables beautifully set with Limoges or antique china.

For starters try sliced rare duck breast on a bed of field greens; grilled lobster with spinach, artichokes, and pasta; or sautéed foie gras with corn crêpes. Sample entrée selections are pan-roasted red snapper with sweet pepper ragout, grilled rack of lamb with crisp potato and Monterey goat cheese, roast loin of rabbit with herb-filled eggplant and basil gnocchi, and pepper charred tuna with grilled vegetable salad. The extensive wine list has over 400 selections. Following dessert, coffee and chocolates are served in the main hall. During the summer guests who are going to Tanglewood can return for a postconcert dessert buffet. Additionally, a tasting menu is available nightly.

Summer lunches at Blantyre are leisurely, with choices such as chilled lobster with sprouts, avocado, and onions; grilled shrimp with saffron pasta; and grilled focaccia with portabello mushrooms.

Open mid-May through October. Twenty-three rooms, suites, and cottages; each with private bath. Rooms, $270–

$500; suites, $300–$700. Children over 12 welcome. Third person $50 additional. 10% gratuity. Continental breakfast included; full breakfast available. Tennis whites required on courts and croquet lawns. Dinner nightly except Monday, mid-May to early November. Prix fixe $70. Lunch (reservations needed) July and August: two courses, $35; three courses, $40. Blantyre Road (off Route 20), P.O. Box 995, Lenox, MA 01240; (413) 637-3556; fax (413) 637-4282; www.blantyre.com.

What to Do.   Facilities at Blantyre include a heated landscaped swimming pool, two tournament-sanctioned bentgrass croquet lawns, four Har-Tru tennis courts, a large indoor hot tub, and a sauna. Golfing is next door at Cranwell. Private guides for fishing or canoeing can be arranged. For concerts go to Tanglewood in Lenox; for dance go to Jacob's Pillow in Beckett; for theater go to Williamstown or to the Berkshire Theatre Festival in Stockbridge. The top museums in the area are the Clark Art Institute, the Norman Rockwell Museum, the Hancock Shaker Village, and Chesterwood.

How to Get There.   From the Massachusetts Turnpike (I-90), take exit 2 at Lee. Go west on Route 20 for 3.1 miles and look for the sign on the right-hand side of the road.

Yankee Clipper Inn

Yankee Clipper Inn, *Rockport, Massachusetts*

An inn that gives you a full ocean view from your room has a magnetic appeal. In our room at the Yankee Clipper we could watch the sun rise, spy seagulls gliding by at eye level, observe lobstermen setting and checking their traps, and fall asleep to the sound of waves lapping against the shore. This prime oceanfront property, a mile north of the center of Rockport in a section called Pigeon Cove, has been owned and operated for more than forty years by the same family. Carrying on the tradition are innkeepers Barbara and Bob Ellis.

Our favorite rooms are located in the three-story building called the Quarterdeck. These rooms have picture windows and are slightly closer to the water than the main inn, so you really have the feeling of being at sea. Although the Oriental Room is not one of the large ones, it is the only room in which you can see the sun rise over the ocean from the bed. Golden State, a thirty-foot-long room with a wall of picture windows, has a queen and a double bed and is the only room on the top floor. Young America, a spacious room on the first floor, has a king-size bed, a living room with a pair of couches, and two picture windows with wonderful ocean views. Neptune's Car, a little smaller than Young America, has two picture windows, one looking toward the main inn and one looking toward the water; a king-size bed; and a private deck with water views. Davy Crockett, on the ground floor of this building, is a new thirty-seven-foot-wide room with ocean views.

The main inn was built in 1929 as a private summer residence. The living room has fine carved molding, a pair of sofas, and a big fireplace. In the winter, guests gather here in the late afternoon to enjoy hot mulled cider and snacks.

We like the big rooms on the third floor in the summer months, as they have open porches and excellent views of the rocky shore. Two rooms with spectacular open private decks are Volunteer, with a king-size bed and lovely Chinese lamps that match the wallpaper, and Sovereign of the Sea, one of the largest rooms, with two antique double sleigh beds.

The best rooms on the second floor have glass-enclosed porches with windows that can be opened. Flying Cloud, the master bedroom in days gone by, has a king-size bed, a chaise longue, and new wicker furniture on the porch. Red Jacket has both a double and a twin bed; the newly winterized porch has floor-to-ceiling windows and antique blue wicker furniture. Sea Witch has a queen-size bed with a fishnet canopy. This room has the largest enclosed porch in the inn and is furnished with a convertible couch and off-white wicker furniture with cushions.

Across the street is the more traditional Bullfinch House, built as a private home in 1840. The rooms here are nicely decorated with antiques, four have baths with whirlpool tubs, but none have close water views. The top choice in this building is Intrepid, with a double whirlpool tub in the bedroom. The Captain's Quarters Villa, a house located nearby, includes three bedrooms, a full bath, a full kitchen, a living room, and a den with a fireplace, and is rented by the week. All the rooms at the inn now have telephones and cable television. The inn has a heated saltwater swimming pool and a rocky bluff, a perfect spot for ocean gazing and watching the lobstermen.

A full breakfast includes a choice of a hot entrée such as blueberry pancakes, poached eggs with spinach basil sauce served in puff pastry, or Belgian waffles with strawberries or other seasonal fruit and whipped cream. Also included is an extensive buffet table of fruit juices, fresh fruit, muffins, sweet breads, and cold cereals.

The Veranda, the restaurant at the Yankee Clipper Inn, is influenced by Tuscan-style cooking. Dining is at tables along a glass wall with spectacular views of the water. Popular dishes on the current menu include Veranda Sole, with layers of Jarlsberg cheese, crabmeat, herbs, and sole; salmon fillet topped with crabmeat and fontina cheese; four-cheese chicken, a boneless breast on pappardelle with four types of cheese; and steamed native lobster. For lighter fare you can order a selection of appetizers such as a pizza, baked stuffed artichoke hearts, or grilled pears on mesclun greens with chèvre cheese and pistachios. Rockport is a dry town, so bring your own bottle of wine.

Twenty-six rooms and suites, each with private bath. Late May to mid-October, $109–$269, or $185–$345 including dinner; other times, $83–$157. Breakfast included. No pets. No smoking. Dinner served nightly 5:30 to 9 P.M. late May to mid-October, fewer days the rest of the year. Entrées $13–$22. Box 2399, 96 Granite Street, Rockport, MA 01966;

(978) 546-3407, (800) 545-3699; fax (978) 546-9730; www. yankeeclipperinn.com.

What to Do. Artists by the hundreds flock to nearby Cape Ann to capture their impressions of this glorious seascape. You'll see many fine examples of their work in the galleries at the Rocky Neck Art Colony, in East Gloucester. The Rockport Art Association has 250 artist members who show their work at different shows throughout the year. The Cape Ann Historical Association, in Gloucester, has a large collection of paintings by Fitz Hugh Lane, the master nautical and luminist painter of the mid-nineteenth century.

Go whale-watching from Gloucester. Tour the medieval-style Hammond Castle that sits on the water's edge and catch an organ recital in the 100-foot-long Great Hall. Browse the shops along Bearskin Neck in Rockport, or relax on one of the white sand beaches in Rockport or Gloucester.

How to Get There. From Boston, take Route 128 north to Cape Ann. Continue on Route 128 through the first traffic circle (first exit for Route 127) and the second traffic circle. Turn left at the next exit (Route 127, Eastern Avenue) and drive 4 miles to Rockport. Continue on Route 127 through Rockport. The road makes a sharp left turn and is now called Granite Street. The inn is about 1.5 miles farther along the road.

The Whalewalk Inn

The Whalewalk Inn, *Eastham, Massachusetts*

From this 1830s whaling master's home located in a residential area of beautifully landscaped old homes, Cape Cod Bay is a five-minute walk, the twenty-seven-mile long Cape Cod Rail Trail is a two-minute bike ride, and the Cape Cod National Seashore is a ten-minute drive. The three-acre property, owned by innkeepers Carolyn and Dick Smith, consists of the main inn and an attached barn as well as a guest cottage and a saltbox cottage.

From the exterior the inn has the charm of old New England, but inside you can see that the Smiths have recently done major remodeling to create open airy rooms, a large landscaped patio where breakfast and afternoon hors d'oeuvres are served, a living room with antiques and a wood-burning fireplace, and a breakfast sunporch. Highly romantic secluded suites, three with wood-burning fireplaces and kitchens, are particularly appealing for a quiet getaway.

The three suites with wood-burning fireplaces are our preference for a romantic stay, particularly early and late in the season when there's a nip in the air. The West Suite, in the guest house, is the largest and is our favorite. A private entrance opens into the particularly spacious living room, which has a cathedral ceiling, two big blue-and-white-striped armchairs designed to be curled up in next to the fireplace, a full kitchen, a dining table, a bedroom with a queen-size bed, and a loft sleeping area over the living room with twin beds. The East Suite, in the same building, has a similar layout except it has a lower ceiling in the living room and does not have a twin-bedded loft. The Saltbox Cottage is set off by itself. This is a single-room lower-ceiling summery country cottage with a queen-size bed, a fireplace, and a Pullman kitchen. We like it a lot because you can lie in bed and look at the fireplace. An outdoor seating area with two chairs and a view of the meadows gives this cottage a private feel.

For a midsummer stay we are also drawn to two other accommodations, one with doors opening onto a deck and the other with doors onto the inn's terrace. The second-floor suite in the barn has an airy large cathedral-ceilinged living room off of which there's a kitchen and a private deck area with a view of the meadows. A separate bedroom has a king-size bed with a blue-and-white quilt. A deluxe first-floor room in the main inn has a particularly feminine feeling with pink walls, a white carpet, a white wicker couch and chairs, a king-size bed with a pink comforter, and a private entrance onto the inn's patio.

The Carriage House, a newly constructed building, has six rooms, each with a gas fireplace, and a mini refrigerator, and all but one with an outdoor patio or deck. The two on the second floor, each twice as large as the four rooms on the first floor, have king-size beds, especially large sitting areas, and large baths with double whirlpool tubs and separate showers. The first-floor rooms have queen-size beds, and one has a double whirlpool tub.

Carolyn and Dick set out hors d'oeuvres such as a vegetable platter, cheeses, and fruit, and provide bar setups. Dick is the breakfast chef. In the summer it is served outside on the brick terrace and at other times in a bright and sunny sunporch set with a large long table or in a second breakfast room set with tables for two or four. The day we stayed we had juice, morning glory muffins, and delicious blueberry and cranberry corn pancakes, the most requested recipe at the inn. Other specialities are Grand Marnier French toast, strawberry shortcake, apple walnut crêpes with ice cream, and Belgian waffles.

Open April through November and selected winter weekends. Sixteen rooms and suites, each with private bath. Memorial Day through Columbus Day, $150–$250; $15–$50 less per night at other times. Breakfast and hors d'oeuvres included. Children over 12 welcome. Third person $30. No smoking. No pets. Two-night minimum on weekends and in season. 220 Bridge Road, Eastham, MA 02642; (508) 255-0617; fax (508) 240-0017; www.whalewalk.com.

Where to Dine.   For fine expensive dining go to Chillingsworth, in Brewster, for a gourmet seven-course prix fixe dinner in elegant surroundings (508) 896-3640) or to High Brewster for less-expensive New American creative fare (508) 896-3636). For fish go to the Brewster Fish House (508) 896-7867). For lobster in a casual setting go to Kadees in East Orleans (508) 255-6184). The Nauset Beach Club, in East Orleans (508) 255-8547), is known for creative northern Italian cuisine. Off the Bay Café, in Orleans (508) 255-5505), has a casual atmosphere and excellent creative continental fare.

Land Ho, in Orleans (508) 255-5165), is the local pub, with burgers, sandwiches, and blackboard specials.

What to Do.   Stop at the Salt Pond Visitors Center of the 40 mile-long Cape Cod National Seashore in Eastham to get detailed maps of beaches, roads, bicycle paths, and walking trails, and a schedule of ranger-led programs. Drive to the Province Lands Visitors Center in Provincetown for views of the illusive Cape Cod light, that mysterious effect caused by the reflections of miles of dunes, moors, and ocean waters that has made this area America's most prolific art colony since the beginning of the twentieth century. Pack a picnic lunch and bike along the 27-mile-long Cape Cod Rail Trail, an old railroad right-of-way that is paved and flat. Visit the 700-acre Massachusetts Audubon Society Wildlife Sanctuary in Wellfleet. Take a whale-watching cruise in Provincetown (April through October). Stroll along 3-mile-long Commercial Street in Provincetown and enjoy the many fine galleries and shops. Visit Chatham, a picture-perfect New England town with lots of shops. Stop at the parking lot just below the lighthouse in Chatham for views of the massive break in the barrier beach.

How to Get There.   Take Route 6 to the Orleans Rotary (about 35 miles from the Sagamore Bridge). Turn left on Rock Harbor Road and take the next right onto Bridge Road to the inn.

Watermark Inn

Watermark Inn, *Provincetown, Massachusetts*

Watermark Inn, located in the quiet residential East End, is perfect if you want to stay directly on the water, watch the sun rise, or listen to the rhythmic pounding of the sea. At high tide the water comes to the edge of the decks outside the rooms, and at low tide the inn has a private sand beach. To your right, you can see the fishing boats and whale-watching boats coming into and departing from Provincetown's harbor. To the left, you can see the lights of Truro and Wellfleet.

The inn is owned by Kevin Shea and Judy Richland, who live and work in Newton during the week. A resident inn-keeper is at the inn in season; during the off-season office hours are greatly reduced. This is the kind of inn where guests are left to their own schedule. Arising early and taking a walk down Commercial Street with a stop for breakfast at one of the coffee shops or Portuguese bakeries, we enjoyed the freedom from planned meals and dining hours. A wide variety of restaurants, markets, and bakeries is within walking distance of the inn.

The sleek, spacious, contemporary suites feature skylights and angled ceilings. The second-floor suites have triangular windows, and furnishings follow crisp, uncluttered Scandinavian style lines. Colorful contemporary designer quilts contrast with the white walls and furniture, which is upholstered in shades of gray and white. Six of the ten suites have sliding glass doors opening onto private decks with full frontal views of the water. Two have working fireplaces that use Duraflame logs. One suite has a full kitchen; each of the others has a kitchenette with a sink, a small refrigerator, a coffeemaker, and a toaster oven.

We favor suites with decks that look out over the water. Our favorite first-floor suite, Suite 3, is the largest and is popular with guests who do not want to climb stairs. Its living room has twelve feet of glass, opening onto the deck with a full frontal water view. Furnishings include a king-size bed and a working fireplace.

The second-floor suites have particularly spectacular water views because of their wider panorama, but the rooms are slightly smaller than those on the first floor. The second-floor deck is set back farther from the water to prevent shading the deck below it. Suite 7, a corner suite, looks west out over Provincetown Harbor. It has a full kitchen and a king-size bed. Suite 8 is a favorite with honeymooners because of its working fireplace, located directly across the room from the queen-size bed. Suite 10, a corner suite with a queen-size bed, faces east—perfect for watching the sunrise. If lying in bed listening to the waves appeals to you, this is the suite where ocean sounds are loudest.

Other suites with full frontal water views and decks are Suite 4 (on the first floor) and Suite 9 (on the second floor). Lower-priced Suites 1 and 2 look out onto an interior courtyard; Suites 5 and 6 have partial water views.

Ten suites, each with private bath. July through early September, $130–$300; other times of the year, $65–$250. Children welcome. $20–40 per additional person, depending on the season. Mid-June to mid-September, one-week minimum stay; two-to-three-night minimum at other times. Meals not included. No pets. 603 Commercial Street, Provincetown, MA 02657;(508) 487-0165; fax (508) 487-2383.

Where to Dine.   The Dancing Lobster (463 Commercial Street; (508) 487-0900), a favorite of ours with windows on three sides of the dining room with great water views, serves imaginative light Italian fare such as Sicilian fish stew served over a large mound of couscous. The Mews (429 Commercial Street; (508) 487-1500), located close to the inn and also with water views on three sides of the dining room, has a more refined feel and serves continental fare. Ciro and Sal's, with exceptional northern Italian cooking, has a large wood-burning fireplace and low ceilings (430 Commercial Street; (508) 487-0049). The tender calamari were sautéed with whole anchovies, lemon, garlic, and cream. Front Street (230 Commercial Street; (508) 487-9715), in the middle of town but not on the water, is another good choice. We particularly liked the leek-and-lobster bisque and the baked artichoke stuffed with bread crumbs and sausage. Try Napi's (7 Freeman Street; (508) 487-1145) for Wellfleet oysters or the Portuguese platter, made with half a lobster, littleneck clams, mussels, fresh fish, and *linguica* sausage smothered in a thick spicy sauce. The Moors (Bradford Street West; (508) 487-0840) has hearty Portuguese soup made with cabbage and spicy *chourico* sausage. Café Edwige (333 Commercial Street; (508) 487-2008) is a good choice for breakfast. The homemade Danish and the frittata with a healthy dose of creative ingredients are favorites.

What to Do. Provincetown is 3 miles long and two to three streets wide. This liberal, closely knit community boasts a fascinating cosmopolitan mix of arts-oriented people. The whale-watching fleet, the largest on the East Coast, attracts many visitors to town, as do (to a lesser extent) the artists and writers who have made this the most famous art colony in the country. There are fine galleries and shops along Commercial Street. The scenery at this tip of Cape Cod is different from anything else you will see in the United States. Fishermen of Portuguese descent leave early each morning in their colorful boats from the end of MacMillan Wharf and return in the afternoon to unload their catches of cod, mackerel, and flounder. Come during any season of the year and nature displays its power along the 40-mile-long Cape Cod National Seashore. Giant sand dunes encroach on the highway near Provincetown. The Province Lands Trail is an 8-mile-long paved bicycle path that goes through the dunes in the Provincetown section of the Cape Cod National Seashore. Race Point and Herring Cove Beaches are nearby. You get a spectacular view of the tip of Cape Cod from the top of the 252-foot-tall Pilgrim Monument, a replica of a Sienna bell tower, and you can see recently discovered pirate treasure in the museum.

How to Get There. From the Bourne or Sagamore Bridges at the beginning of the Cape, take Route 6 directly to

Provincetown and turn left at the first exit, which is marked East End. Turn right onto Route 6A. Bear left at the fork onto Commercial Street. Stay on the water-side road. The inn is on the left less than 1 mile down the road.

A guest room at Land's End Inn

Land's End Inn, *Provincetown, Massachusetts*

Sitting on a hilltop at the far west end of Provincetown, with panoramic views of the harbor, the bay, and the dunes, this is a one-of-a-kind turreted Victorian bungalow. The common areas are decorated and overflowing with the extensive glass collection of the late innkeeper, David Schoolman, who spent twenty years building and decorating this ornate structure. The innkeeper now is Anthony Arakelian. Common areas include the solarium, with a curved picture window overlooking the bay, and the atmospherically lit living room, with a stone fireplace, overstuffed easy chairs, Tiffany-style lamps, stained-glass window, and exotic wood carvings. The walls throughout the inn are covered with lots and lots of paintings.

Our favorite rooms are those on the upper levels with the best views. The loft duplex suite with four outside deck areas is the ultimate. The lower level is a large living room with picture windows, and a kitchen; the huge bathroom has a high ceiling and both a double whirlpool tub on a raised platform and a stall shower. A spiral staircase leads to the upper-level sleeping loft, which has a queen-size bed and fantastic harbor views. This room has 500 square feet of decking plus an observation tower with table and chairs that is 186 feet above sea level. In the New Tower Room, with almost a 360-degree view, the queen-size bed is situated under a cupola that is lined with rare African wood and blue glass. A wraparound deck off this room affords a fabulous view. The Library, a large room on the main floor with a great view of the water and the gardens and a private wraparound deck, is another favorite. The Old Tower Room, with the feel of an elegant imaginary hashish den, is most unusual. It features an almost-round queen-size bed, Oriental rugs, and a Turkish brazier that hangs from the peaked dark-wood-paneled ceiling. All the rooms are highly decorated with a great deal of visual appeal and are wonderfully eccentric.

Each of the garden-level rooms and apartments has a private entrance offering more privacy. The French Country Apartment, the larger of the two, has a living room with a trundlebed sofa and a kitchenette, a separate bedroom with a queen-size bed, and sliding doors opening off the living room and onto the garden. The English Garden Room, on this level, is a large room with good views of the garden. NOTE: Rooms have fans (no air-conditioning), and all but three have baths (most fairly small) with showers only.

For breakfast, available from 8 to 11 A.M., guests help themselves to a buffet of juice, muffins, and bakery-made fruit breads that can be toasted. You can sit at one of the tables or take a tray and sit on the porch, by the fireplace, in the solarium, or outside by the lily pond. Don't forget your book, your sketch pad, or your paintbrushes; you won't find another inn even remotely like this.

Sixteen rooms and a loft suite, fifteen with private bath, including two efficiency apartments. Memorial Day through September, private bath rooms $110–$190; loft suite $285, shared bath rooms $85; off-season, $65–165, $165, loft suite $185. Continental breakfast included. Infants and children over 9 welcome, $25 additional. No pets. No smoking. Five-to-seven-night minimum stay July through first week of September; two-night weekend minimum (except holidays) at other times. 22 Commercial Street, Provincetown, MA 02657; (508) 487-0706; (800) 276-7088.

Where to Dine.   The Dancing Lobster (463 Commercial Street; (508) 487-0900), a favorite of ours with windows on three sides of the dining room with great water views, serves imaginative light Italian fare such as Sicilian fish stew served over a large mound of couscous. The Mews (429 Commercial Street; (508) 487-1500), with water views on three sides of the dining room, has a more refined feel and serves continental fare. Ciro and Sal's, with exceptional northern Italian cooking, has a large wood-burning fireplace and low ceilings (430 Commercial Street; (508) 487-0049). Front Street (230 Commercial Street; (508) 487-9715), in the middle of town but not on the water, is another good choice. Try Napi's (7 Freeman Street; (508) 487-1145) for Wellfleet oysters or the Portuguese platter, made with half a lobster, littleneck clams, mussels, fresh fish, and *linguica* sausage smothered in a thick spicy sauce. The Moors, which is near the inn (Bradford Street West; (508)

487-0840), has hearty Portuguese soup made with cabbage and spicy *chourico* sausage.

What to Do. Provincetown is 3 miles long and two to three streets wide. This liberal, closely knit community boasts a fascinating cosmopolitan mix of arts-oriented people. The whale-watching fleet, the largest on the East Coast, attracts many visitors to town, as do (to a lesser extent) the artists and writers who have made this the most famous art colony in the country. There are fine galleries and shops along Commercial Street. The scenery at this tip of Cape Cod is different from anything else you will see in the United States. Fishermen of Portuguese descent leave early each morning in their colorful boats from the end of MacMillan Wharf and return in the afternoon to unload their catches of cod, mackerel, and flounder. Come during any season of the year and nature displays its power along the 40-mile-long Cape Cod National Seashore. Giant sand dunes encroach on the highway near Provincetown. The Province Lands Trail is an 8-mile-long paved bicycle path that goes through the dunes in the Provincetown section of the Cape Cod National Seashore. Race Point and Herring Cove Beaches are nearby. You get a spectacular view of the tip of Cape Cod from the top of the 252-foot-tall Pilgrim Monument, a replica of a Sienna bell tower, and you can see recently discovered pirate treasure in the museum.

How to Get There. From the Bourne or Sagamore Bridges at the beginning of the Cape, take Route 6 directly to Provincetown. The inn is at the far end of Commercial Street.

The Charlotte Inn

The Charlotte Inn, *Edgartown, Martha's Vineyard, Massachusetts*

For lovers of superb antiques, the Charlotte Inn, a magnificent complex of five buildings tied together with brick courtyards and refined English gardens, is the crown jewel of Martha's Vineyard lodgings. The inn is located in Edgartown one block from the water on a quiet street of elegant nineteenth-century homes, brick sidewalks, and large shade trees. Gery Conover has owned the inn since 1970. He and his wife, Paula, live in the main building and over the years have purchased or constructed the adjacent properties. The main building was built in 1860 for Captain Samuel Osborne. The Summer House, with a porch that overlooks one of the gardens, is where tea is served in the summer. The 1705 Garden House is across the street and has a cozy living room parlor with a fireplace. The two newer buildings are the Carriage House and the Coach House, both located behind the main inn.

This is an inn for the perfectionist. The first floor of the inn is a series of four parlors that also serve as exhibit space for the Conovers' art gallery. Everywhere you look there is another perfectly fashioned vignette, a photographer's dream: a desk from a barrister's office in Scotland, equestrian prints and oils, bronze sculptures, English riding boots, and hundreds of volumes of leather-bound books throughout the inn. All the common rooms, outdoor seating areas, and guest rooms have a selection of current upscale magazines.

The most sumptuous accommodation is the Coach House Suite. This is the entire second floor above the museumlike garage that houses two operating antique automobiles, one a 1939 Ford Woodie station wagon that Paula and Gery drive during the summer. The high-peaked-ceilinged sitting room has a large Palladian window with a window seat, an English marble gas fireplace, easy chairs, and over 300 leather-bound volumes. The bedroom is enormous, with a king-size bed covered with beautiful lace linens, a pair of matching easy chairs, and antique dressers. What a perfect spot for a honeymoon! The suite on the second floor of the Carriage House is the second most luxurious accommodation. The sitting room has a green damask couch, two easy chairs, and a fireplace. The bedroom has a queen-size four-poster bed situated so you can lie in bed and look down on the gardens.

Other favorites are Room 14, in the Summer House, a large room with a white baby grand piano (not tuned), a fireplace set with two easy chairs, and a queen-size four-poster bed. Room 21 in the Garden House, is a top pick in the summer as you can lie in the queen-size bed, and look through the French doors to view a picture-perfect scene of the gardens, the perennial borders, and the Conovers' little garden cottage. Room 12, one of the large fireplaced rooms in the main inn, has a queen-size English mahogany canopied paneled bed and windows on three sides of the room. Most of the rooms have televisions tucked into armoires and antique-looking telephones in keeping with the period.

Breakfast of fresh squeezed orange juice and pastries, croissants, bagels, and toast is included. Daily specials such as stuffed French toast, an egg dish, or pancakes are available at an additional coast.

L'étoile at the Charlotte Inn is our favorite restaurant on Martha's Vineyard. The dining room was created from a brick-and-flagstone patio that was enclosed and then decorated with prints and oil paintings, Boston ferns, and large terra-cotta pots holding ficus trees. There is also a small outdoor summer dining area that's very popular. Tables are set with silver, Limoges china, and a single red rose. Our dinner included seared veal sweetbreads with baby beets and endive in puff pastry and a chowder made with roasted tomatoes, mussels, littlenecks, and scallops flavored with a dab or two of curry mayonnaise. For an intermezzo you have a choice of sorbet (we had grape sorbet, served with a bunch of champagne grapes) or a salad of local baby greens. There is always a lobster preparation available. We had a delicious and creative etuvée of lobster and scallops. The lobster is cooked in tamari; mixed with scallops, corn, and sea greens; and then put back in the shell. A second excellent choice was roasted double rib lamb chops topped with a rich roasted eggplant and port wine sauce accompanied by a phyllo tart filled with goat cheese and chestnuts. For dessert we chose the frozen biscuit glacé, composed of two layers of hazelnut meringue with Frangelico ice cream and cappuccino sauce.

Twenty-three rooms and two suites, each with private bath, five with fireplaces. May (weekends) and June through October, rooms $275–$495, suites $495–$750; other times, rooms

$165–$395, suites $395–$550. Continental breakfast included; full breakfast is available at an extra charge. Children over 14 welcome. Rooms are double occupancy only. No pets. Two-night minimum on weekends. Dinner nightly in season; weekends and some weekdays off-season, 6:30 to 9:45 P.M. Prix fixe $58–$65. South Summer Street, Edgartown, MA 02539; (508) 627-4751; fax (508) 627-4652.

What to Do. During the summer the beaches are the big attraction. Take a walking tour of Edgartown to see whaling captains' homes, old churches, and the Vineyard Museum. In Oak Bluffs, look at the Carpenter Gothic cottages and ride the Flying Horses Carousel. Drive up-island to Menemsha, a fishing village, and to Gay Head to the lighthouse and the cliffs. For hiking try one of the wildlife sanctuaries such as Menemsha Hills, Felix Neck, or Cedar Tree Neck.

How to Get There. Ferries leave from Woods Hole year-round and seasonally from Falmouth, New Bedford, and Hyannis. Reservations to take your car in summer months are a must and should be made well in advance. There are flights from Boston, Hyannis, Nantucket, and New Bedford.

Bob Schellhammer

Room 1 at Thorncroft Inn

Thorncroft Inn, *Vineyard Haven, Martha's Vineyard, Massachusetts*

If you've ever fantasized about soaking in your own six-person hot tub in the privacy of your own room, you have found the right place. Karl and Lynn Buder's inn is located in a prime residential area 1 mile from the Vineyard Haven ferry, an advantage because you can get to the inn without a car. To preserve the privacy of guests, the front door of the inn is kept locked at all times.

For a romantic stay the favorites are the two rooms with the large hot tubs and Room 15, a cottage with a garage, which offers total privacy. Room 1, in the main house, has an 1855 queen-size bed with a carved walnut eight-foot headboard, matching eight-foot marble topped dresser, and a wood-burning fireplace. A door opens into another room where there is a 300-gallon six-person hot tub that's kept at 104 degrees. The Carriage House, down a path behind the inn, is the setting for more rooms and a second hot tub room, Room 10, with a 265-gallon six-person tub. The adjacent bedroom has a 1790 queen-size canopy bed that faces the wood-burning fireplace. And, in case you're wondering . . . the water is changed after every guest. The newest room is the Cottage, a private space surrounded by trees. The Cottage is fifty-two feet by twenty-six feet with a garage and a private deck with a hammock and Adirondack furniture. The bedroom has a king-size canopy bed (the only one in the inn). The living room has a two-person whirlpool tub that is arranged so you can see the fireplace while you relax in the tub. The Cottage has a full bath with a double sink and an oversize shower, as well as a powder room.

In the Carriage House we like Rooms 9 and 14, both suites with wood-burning fireplaces and two-person whirlpool tubs. It is matter of personal preference as to which to pick. Room 14 has the whirlpool in the living room, so you can lie in the tub and look at the fireplace, and a bedroom with a queen-size canopy bed. Room 9 is the same but the bedroom has a queen-size canopy bed and a wood-burning fireplace, and the double whirlpool tub is in the large bath. Favorites on the second floor of the Carriage House are Room 11, with a fireplace and a two-person shower with dual shower heads, and Room 12, with a queen-size canopy bed. Both rooms have private decks.

While these are the most sumptuous rooms, there are ten rooms with wood-burning fireplaces, many with fishnet canopy beds, and others with decks looking into the woods or the backyard. All the rooms have queen-size beds (except the Cottage, which has a king-size bed), phones, and televisions, and most have refrigerators. The buildings are centrally air-conditioned.

Breakfast seatings are at 8:15 and 9:30 A.M., with a different entrée served each day. A booklet in each room describes the exact menu for each day of the week—such as cheese strata and sausages on Friday, almond French toast on Monday, and herb quiche with a large plate of cut fruit on Sunday. Lighter options such as a fruit plate, granola, soft-boiled eggs, or shredded wheat are also available if you let the Buders know the night before. If you want to sleep late they will deliver a breakfast tray of juice, fruit, yogurt, and a selection of muffins, scones, or bagels to your room at 9 or 10 A.M. Tea and a plate of pastries are available from 4 to 5 P.M. Turndown service includes white chocolate truffles.

Karl and Lynn are extraordinarily well organized and have an extensive booklet in each room with menus and answers to every question one could possibly have, maps of the island, things to do, and restaurant suggestions.

Fourteen rooms, each with private bath. Late June through Labor Day, $200–$450; other times of the year, $160–$425. Breakfast and tea included. Not appropriate for children. Rooms are double occupancy only. No smoking. No pets. 460 Main Street, P.O. Box 1022, Vineyard Haven, MA 02568; (508) 693-3333, (800) 332-1236; fax (508) 693-5419; www. thorncroft.com.

Where to Dine.   L'Etoile at the Charlotte Inn in Edgartown (27 South Summer Street; (508) 627-4751) is our favorite fine dining restaurant, with a beautiful garden setting. In Vineyard Haven the top restaurant is Le Grenier (Upper Main Street; (508) 693-4906), which serves classic country French dishes. The Black Dog Tavern (Beach Street Extension; (508) 693-9223), also in Vineyard Haven, next to the ferry, is an island institution with lots of character. The Sweet Life Café, in Oak Bluffs (Upper Circuit Avenue; (508) 696-0200), serving creative new American fare, is located in a Victorian house.

For lobster-in-the-rough and dramatic sunset views drive out to the Homeport, in Menemsha. (North Road; (508) 645-2679), but be prepared to wait in the summer.

What to Do. During the summer the beaches are the big attraction. Take a walking tour of Edgartown to see whaling captains' homes, old churches, and the Vineyard Museum. In Oak Bluffs, look at the Carpenter Gothic cottages and ride the Flying Horses Carousel. Drive up-island to Menemsha, a fishing village, and to Gay Head to the lighthouse and the cliffs. For hiking try one of the wildlife sanctuaries such as Menemsha Hills, Felix Neck, or Cedar Tree Neck.

How to Get There. Ferries leave from Woods Hole year-round and seasonally from Falmouth, New Bedford, and Hyannis. Reservations to take your car in summer months are a must and should be made well in advance. There are flights from Boston, Hyannis, Nantucket, and New Bedford.

The Wauwinet

The Wauwinet, *Nantucket, Massachusetts*

Situated between the Atlantic Ocean and Nantucket Bay, some 9 miles from town, this full-service world-class inn owned by Stephen and Jill Karp allows guests to soak in the healthful sea breezes with nary a care. Walking through the lobby, the library/lounge, the hallways, and the guests' rooms of this inn is like turning the pages of *Architectural Digest.* Innkeepers Russ and Debbie Cleveland have made this inn into one of the great East Coast destinations. Quality and good taste without a trace of stuffy or pompous formality are omnipresent. Relish the exquisite bouquets of fresh flowers, gorgeous chintz fabrics, whimsical trompe l'oeil floors, antique scrimshaw, original elephant folio Audubon prints, fine oil paintings, and bronze sculptures. The list could go on and on, as no expense has been spared to create this magnificent showplace.

Each of the rooms is individually decorated, with designer sheets and comforters, many with antique pine armoires and chests, Berber rugs, baskets, old hatboxes, wood carvings, bronze sculptures, and books about Nantucket. All the rooms have air-conditioning, phones, robes, CDs, TV/VCRs, and refrigerators upon request. While all of the rooms are designed with the same attention to detail, the variation in price is determined by the size of the room and the view. The less expensive rooms have queen-size beds (except for one with twin beds) and overlook the front of the inn. Bay-view rooms are larger, and the deluxe rooms all have king-size beds or two queen-size beds with panoramic views of the inn's beach and the bay—and some also have a partial view of the ocean.

In addition to the twenty-nine rooms in the main inn, there are also five cottages, each boasting the same designer country feel as the main inn. Idlewild A, a one-bedroom cottage with a cathedral ceiling, and the Anchorage, a four-bedroom, three-bath cottage with a kitchenette, are the two cottages with wood-burning fireplaces. Idlewild B, a two-bedroom cottage with a living room, has a full kitchen. The other three cottages each have two connecting units with a bedroom and bath.

A full breakfast menu, available from 8 to 10:30 A.M., and brunch on Sunday are included in the room rate. Fresh squeezed orange or grapefruit juice, berries, cereals, hot entrées including wild turkey hash with poached eggs and hollandaise, eggs Benedict or Argyle, egg white omelettes, pancakes, and French toast are options.

There are no additional charges for use of the tennis courts, sunfish and rowing shells, mountain bikes, or the inn's collection of 450 videotapes (accompanied by complimentary fresh-popped popcorn). Sit on the lawn or in the inn's library, with a wood-burning fireplace and stocked with good books (guests are welcome to borrow a book if they haven't finished reading it by the end of their stay); swim or stroll along miles of pristine beaches. Russ takes guests on four-wheel-drive natural history excursions to Great Point, a highlight of our stay, and the inn's classic Woody is used to take guests on tours of Siasconset (which the locals pronounce 'Sconset). A free jitney service runs into town on a regular schedule.

From mid-May to mid-June and from late September through October the inn has complimentary weekday excursions such as the lobster cruise that we took. There are also excursions to learn about constructing lightship baskets, tours and tastings at Nantucket Vineyard, shell fishing, surf-casting or charter-boat fishing (for an additional fee), and botanical walks of the magnificently landscaped property. In the fall you can also dig for scallops and pick cranberries, learn about their history, and have the chef prepare a dish using your catch.

If we could dine at only one of the fine restaurants on Nantucket, Topper's at the Wauwinet is definitely the one we'd choose. The two summery dining rooms are filled with fresh flowers, well-spaced couches and upholstered chairs, a wood-burning fireplace for chilly evenings, bronze sculptures, and oil paintings. The menu features imaginative American cuisine that draws on the best of the country's regional specialties. The presentation of the dishes is dramatic, with creatively shaped china and glassware complementing the dishes. The sparkling mineral water served at dinner is complimentary. For the ultimate in appetizers try the Osetra or Beluga caviar, served on a long Annie glass tray with the usual accompaniments—and, if desired, with iced vodka or champagne. A black plate offsets the generous portion of seared rare coriander-encrusted tuna set on soba noodles with slivered marinated vegetables. A longtime favorite is the crab cakes—a combination of jumbo lump crabmeat and lobster meat gar-

nished with smoked corn. Seared foie gras comes with rhu-
barb marmalade and toasted brioche.

The lobster fettuccine is an impressive dish we'll long re-
member both for its flavor and for its presentation on a long
narrow white platter. The fresh noodles are mixed with shiitake mushrooms, asparagus spears, and a bit of lobster-
flavored cream, and at either end are large pieces of
pan-roasted lobster. The cod comes from Chatham and is
served atop beets, lobster, and leeks. Leg of lamb with morel
mushrooms and fiddleheads; veal chop with gnocchi, peas,
and artichokes; and filet mignon with vidalia onion mashed
potatoes are all excellent. The filet mignon, arctic char, and
veal chops are broiled over applewood charcoal. The restaurant recently received the prestigious Wine Spectator Grand
Award of Excellence, one of two on the island and in a league
of about sixty in the country.

Be sure to have dessert. The rich molten chocolate cake
with a warm chocolate center and a scoop of ice cream was
pure delight, as was the trio of intensely flavored sorbets, for
a lighter ending. A selection of cookies and candies comes
with your coffee.

On a nice day, have lunch or light fare and a specialty drink
on the patio, which has a view of the grounds and the water.
The menu is designed so you can sample three, four, or five
small portions, priced by the number of items selected. Tuna
tartare with a nori baguette, a lobster club sandwich on
toasted brioche, wild turkey hash, smoked salmon rosette
with Osetra caviar, and grilled portabello mushrooms and asparagus with goat cheese are some of the selections.

Open early May through late October. Thirty-five rooms
and suites, each with private bath. Mid-June to mid-
September, rooms $310–$710, cottage suites $610–$1,400;
mid-May to mid-June and mid-September through late

October, rooms $195–$590, cottage suites $490–$1,170. Breakfast and afternoon sherry and cheese included. Children welcome. Rooms are double occupancy only. No pets. No smoking. Minimum up to four nights depending on the season and days of the week. Breakfast, Sunday brunch, lunch, afternoon light fare, and dinner daily. Lunch entrées $20–$27. Dinner entrées $29–$49. Complimentary lunch and dinner cruises for diners leaving from Nantucket Town, mid-June through mid-September, by reservation. Box 2580, 120 Wauwinet Road, Nantucket, MA 02584; (508) 228-0145, (800) 426-8718; fax (508) 228-6712; www.wauwinet.com.

What to Do. The Wauwinet will arrange for its skipper to take you to an isolated spot on Coatue, a remote part of the island, where you can enjoy the privacy of the beach and a custom-created gourmet picnic. Bicycle to Siasconset or to Madaket on the bicycle paths. Take walks at Sanford Farm and Tupancy Links, land owned by the Conservation Foundation. Walk the streets in town and shop at the designer boutiques, galleries, and craft stores. The Historical Association has restored twelve buildings that are open to the public. Be sure to visit the Whaling Museum, the Peter Foulger Museum, and Hadwen House.

How to Get There. The ferry from Hyannis takes two hours and twenty minutes. If you plan to bring a car be sure to get advance reservations, especially for the peak summer season. The Hy-Line Cruise from Hyannis, a passenger line only, takes one hour and forty-five minutes. The M.V. *Grey Lady*, a water jet catamaran, makes the trip in one hour. From May through October the Freedom Cruise Line, a passenger line, leaves from Harwich Port. Flights leave from Hyannis, Boston, Providence, and Newark.

Cliffside Inn

Cliffside Inn, *Newport, Rhode Island*

This bay-windowed turreted Victorian, built at the turn of the century, is located on a quiet residential street about a fifteen-minute walk from the harbor area and just down the road from the famed Cliff Walk. The mansion is filled with breathtaking rooms and suites, all with phones, televisions, and VCRs (there is a library of more than 100 movies for guests' use). Eleven rooms have both fireplaces and double whirlpools. The innkeeper is Stephan Nicolas. Throughout the house are more than 100 copies or originals of paintings by Beatrice Turner, a reclusive painter who painted over 3,000 works, including more than 1,000 self-portraits. Turner lived here until her death in 1948.

Each time we visit we find that Win Baker, the owner, has been busy with a new construction project. The two-level Garden Suite, with an entrance off the front porch, is a spectacular space. The upper floor has a fireplace, a queen-size bed, and a narrow iron spiral staircase leading to the lower level, which is forty-three feet long from the reading nook to the end of the private enclosed patio garden. The entire floor is stunning pink Peruvian limestone and is radiant heated, and the room has a whirlpool (the largest double whirlpool in the inn) that faces a second fireplace. Glass doors close off the bath, which includes an oversize shower.

The Tower Suite has a private entrance, a first-floor bath with a double whirlpool and a separate marble shower, and a second floor with a queen-size bed, a fireplace, a window seat, and a twenty-five foot turret tower with a cupola. The Governor's Suite has the largest bedroom in the inn, with a California king-size bed, a living room, and a double-sided fireplace that you can see from the bed and from the double whirlpool. An antique birdcage shower sprays water out of four bars that encircle the shower.

Miss Beatrice's Room has the best winter water view. The bedroom has a queen-size bed and a fireplace. The bath is as large as many rooms, with a double whirlpool set in front of the bay window and a separate double-headed shower. The Turner Suite has skylights in all three rooms: a separate sitting room with a green marble fireplace, a bedroom, and a bath with a double whirlpool tub.

The Seaview Cottage started as a ranch-style house that was totally gutted and made into two spectacular suites with cathedral ceilings. Guests staying here can have breakfast served in the sitting room in this building, on the porch, or in the inn. The Cliff Suite, the larger of the two, has a bedroom with a king-size bed and a double-sided fireplace that is also visible from the large living room; a small study with a fireplace, a stereo, and a fax; and a bath with a double whirlpool. The Atlantic Suite has a queen-size pine bed, a high-ceilinged living room with a fieldstone fireplace, and a bath with a double whirlpool tub and separate shower.

Even the lower-priced, smaller rooms without the whirlpools are lovely, and each exhibits the same attention to detail as is found in the larger, more sumptuous rooms. A few we particularly like are the Library Room, which has a fireplace, and Miss Healy's and Miss Emily's Rooms, each with baths with showers only.

A Victorian tea, set out from 4:30 to 5:30 P.M. should not be missed. The lace-draped table is artfully arranged with a silver teapot, pitchers of ice tea or lemonade, a decanter of sherry, tiered plates of superb pastries including eclairs, tarts, scones, tea sandwiches, cookies, and cake, all of which are made by the inn's chef. You can have your tea by the fireplace in the parlor or on the wicker-filled front porch, or you can take a plate back to the privacy of your own fantasy room. At turndown they leave homemade chocolates and a card with the next day's weather.

Your day begins in a civilized fashion when a tray of coffee or tea, juice, and your choice of about a dozen newspapers is brought to your room anytime from 7 to 9 A.M. A full breakfast is served from 8 to 10 A.M. in the parlor at two large tables or in season on the porch. Guests help themselves to the buffet of juice, fruit, cereal, and bakery items and are served a different hot dish daily. On our most recent visit it was a croissant sandwich with scrambled eggs and sausage, at other times it has been banana-filled crêpes, eggs Benedict, and almond French toast.

Fifteen rooms and suites, each with private bath. $185–$425. Breakfast and afternoon tea included. Children over 13 welcome. Third person $30 additional. No smoking. No pets. Two-to-three-night weekend minimum. 2 Seaview Avenue, Newport, RI 02840; (401) 847-1811, (800) 845-1811; fax (401) 848-5850; www.cliffsideinn.com.

Where to Dine. For casual dining we can't get enough of the lasagna di verdure or the sweet red roasted peppers in oil and garlic at Puerini's (24 Memorial Boulevard, Newport; (401) 847-5506). At Scales and Shells (527 Thames Street, Newport; (401) 846-FISH) don't miss the lobster fra diavolo. The thick, spicy tomato sauce peppered with clams, mussels, squid, and lobster is served on a bed of linguine and comes to your table in a steaming hot frying pan. For lunch or an afternoon snack get a bowl of thick pasta fagioli with Parmesan cheese and a cappuccino at Ocean Coffee Roaster (22 Washington Square, Newport; (401) 846-6060). Creative new American cuisine is best at the Place at Yesterday's (28 Washington Square, Newport; (401 847-0116). The Commodore Room at the Black Pearl on Bannister's Wharf (401) 846-5264) still requires a jacket for men and has an outstanding wine list. White Horse Tavern (Marlborough and Farewell Streets; (401) 849-3600) is where you will dine in the atmosphere of America's oldest tavern, built in 1687. Try the grilled lamb or veal chops.

What to Do. Newport is an area that you can return to time and again. If you choose, you can spend your entire visit indoors touring the mansions. The Breakers is the most opulent. Others along Bellevue Avenue include Marble House, Chateau-sur-Mer, the Elms, Rosecliff, Kingscote, and Belcourt Castle. The 3.5-mile Cliff Walk is one of the most famous in America. On one side is a row of mansions like none other in existence, and on the other the mighty Atlantic pounds the rocky shoreline at your feet. The experience, especially the day after a storm, is unforgettable. You can head to the beach. Drive or bike along 10-mile-long Ocean Drive and see more mansions, grand estates, and dramatic ocean views. Stop at Hammersmith Farm to see Jacqueline Bouvier Kennedy Onassis's childhood bedroom and the office that President

John F. Kennedy used as his summer home away from Washington. Go to the 1759 Touro Synagogue, the first in the colonies. Go antiquing, gallery hopping, and shopping. Take a harbor cruise or rent a sailboat. Or you can simply plop yourself down near the water, watch the waves, and take the time to enjoy a good book.

How to Get There.   From Boston, take I-93 south, then Route 24 south to Route 114 south to Newport. Turn left on Memorial Drive, right on Cliff Avenue, left on Seaview Avenue. From New York City, take I-95 north to Rhode Island. Exit at Route 138 east into Newport. Turn left off Memorial Drive onto Cliff Avenue, left on Seaview Avenue.

Onne Van Der Wal

Castle Hill Inn and Resort

Castle Hill Inn and Resort, *Newport, Rhode Island*

This rambling 1874 shingled Victorian mansion, located 5 miles from the center of the Newport tourist scene on a 40-acre peninsula overlooking the Atlantic Ocean, has one of the finest locations on the East Coast. In the morning you wake to the muffled crash of the surf against the rocks. Outside your window a private view of the yachts sailing in and out of Newport Harbor waits to greet you. A deep foghorn warns mariners from the working lighthouse on the property.

The first floor of the inn includes four dining rooms, a lounge that commands an impressive view of the water, and a lobby sitting room.

Be aware that there are dramatic variations in the size and type of accommodations. Our overwhelming first choice would be one of the six large rooms that face the water, the suite, and the first-floor suite in the chalet. Room 6, the Bridal

Suite, has a king-size bed with a draped crown, a large bay window offering full-frontal panoramic water views, and a bath with an antique bathtub and separate shower. Room 7 is completely wood-paneled, including the ceiling, and has two queen-size sleigh beds. Room 9, the Turret Room, on the third floor, has a king-size Victorian bed and a full-frontal water view from the circular turret windows. Room 10, a suite with no water views, has a very large sitting room with a white brocade sofa, and a wood-paneled bedroom with a king-size bed. The three small rooms that share a bath and a half have been renovated but are not a top choice as they are over the kitchen. The smells are not a problem if you keep the windows shut or use the air conditioner. All the rooms now have down comforters, terry cloth bathrobes, and phones, and there are televisions in many of the rooms. The side rooms that do not get the breeze from the water have air conditioners.

The chalet, formerly the laboratory of the original owner, Dr. Agassiz, was redecorated and is generally rented to a family or used for business meetings. The first floor is a magnificent suite that includes a full kitchen, a large living room, and a bedroom. The second floor has four tiny bedrooms, one with a private bath and three that share a second bath.

Harbor House, a building with six units with porches with water views, was totally transformed and is now just as popular as rooms in the main inn. Each unit has both a front and back porch where you can sit and look at Narragansett Bay, a king-size bed, a gas fireplace, and a bath with a single-size whirlpool tub.

For those who want to stay right on the water and hear the waves crashing on the beach in their own cottage with a deck and cooking facilities and don't mind rustic accommodations, the beach cottages are perfect. They are working on these. All have been freshened up, and they are starting to do major transformations to about eight of the cottages.

The first floor of the inn has been completely refurbished. The rich butternut and pine woodwork was cleaned and lightened, new carpets and furniture were added, and three wood-burning fireplaces (in the lobby, lounge, and Agassiz Dining Room) add a warm inviting feel during the colder months. Of the four dining rooms our preference is the Sunset Room, a curved bright room with large windows on three sides, giving you the feeling that you are on a ship looking out in all directions at the water, as well as the outdoor terrace with water views.

For lunch we sat outside and enjoyed the breeze, the water views, and the lobster salad served in a croissant. Lunch is also served indoors with selections such as planked salmon, lobster and halibut stew, or grilled turkey breast or burger. On Sundays there's a very popular and very crowded jazz brunch, often with lines of people waiting to be seated (no reservations). In the summer grilled food is also served outside. It is quite a happening here on a summer weekend.

Entrées from the dinner menu include a lobster preparation such as sautéed lobster with pappardelle pasta, spicy lobster thermidor, or lobster fricasse. Other selections from recent menus include grilled tuna, braised rabbit with chanterelles, grilled sirloin and a Maine crab cake, and barbecue-smoked duck with green chile cheese grits. During the quiet season a smaller fireside inn menu is served that includes choices such as grilled skirt steak on a baguette or sautéed lobster and mussels on cornmeal waffles.

Twenty-one inn, chalet, and Harbor House rooms and suites, fifteen with private bath. June through October, $115–$325; other times, $75–$225. Two night weekend minimum. Eighteen beach cottages. $900–$1,100 weekly. Available nightly in the off-season. Breakfast and afternoon tea included except in the cottages. Children over 12 welcome in the inn. No pets. Two-to-three-night weekend minimum. Lunch or brunch and dinner daily. November through March, closed on Monday and Tuesday. Lunch entrées $7–$12. Brunch entrées $11–$22. Dinner entrées $16–$27 (lobster and rack of lamb $30–$42). Ocean Drive, Newport, RI 02840; (401) 849-3800, (888) 466-1355; fax (401) 849-3838; www.castlehill inn.com.

What to Do.   Newport is an area that you can return to time and again. If you choose, you can spend your entire visit indoors touring the mansions. The Breakers is the most opulent. Others along Bellevue Avenue include Marble House, Chateau-sur-Mer, the Elms, Rosecliff, Kingscote, and Belcourt Castle. The 3.5 mile Cliff Walk is one of the most famous in America. On one side is a row of mansions like none other in existence, and on the other the mighty Atlantic pounds the rocky shoreline at your feet. The experience, especially the day after a storm, is unforgettable. You can head to the beach. Drive or bike along 10-mile-long Ocean Drive and see more mansions, grand estates, and dramatic ocean views. Stop at Hammersmith Farm to see Jacqueline Bouvier Kennedy Onassis's childhood bedroom and the office that President John F. Kennedy used as his summer home away from Washington. Go to the 1759 Touro Synagogue, the first in the colonies. Go antiquing, gallery hopping, and shopping. Take a harbor cruise or rent a sailboat. Or you can simply plop yourself down near the water, watch the waves, and take the time to enjoy a good book.

How to Get There.   From Boston, take I-93 south, then Route 24 south to Route 114 south to Newport. Follow Thames Street. Turn right on Wellington Avenue. From this point on take every available right. After going past the Coast Guard Station the road turns sharply to the right and then to the left. The driveway is on the right. From New York City, take I-95 north to Route 138 east. After you cross the bridge follow signs to the center of Newport and Thames Street. Then follow the above directions.

The Windsor Suite at Elm Tree Cottage

Elm Tree Cottage, *Newport, Rhode Island*

The amount of common space for the guests is extraordinary in this large gray-shingle-style mansion built in 1882 on a street of large homes overlooking Easton Pond, two blocks from the beach. The innkeepers are Tom and Priscilla Malone. The large living room has a wall of windows overlooking the back gardens, a pair of white couches, two pianos (a Steinway baby grand as well as an upright baby grand), and a table with a jigsaw puzzle in progress. The adjoining morning room, a comfortable place to read the newspaper and have an early cup of coffee, is more casual, with wicker furniture covered with pillows. Be sure to notice the two round stained-glass windows in the pub and the stained-glass pieces throughout the home, all of which were made by the Malones. The pub, constructed by a former owner to resemble the interior cabin of a 1930s yacht, has a unique mirror and bar top decorated with 1921 silver dollars. Guests can help themselves to soft drinks whenever they like.

The Windsor Suite, a huge 1,000-square-foot room overlooking the back of the inn, with a carved Louis XV headboard and a crown canopy, a king-size bed, a fireplace, a television, a CD player, and a large bath with a vanity dressing table and crystal chandelier, is truly a sumptuous room.

Room 4, with a fireplace, a sitting area, and a king-size bed with an upholstered French headboard, is the second most requested room. Room 5 has a king-size bed, French carved cornices over the windows, a fireplace, and a bath with a double-size soaking tub. Room 2 has a more masculine equestrian feel with a fireplace, a queen-size bed, and a bath with a shower and separate tub. Room 3, a smaller, more feminine room, has a queen-size mahogany bed with a canopy crown. The Library, a first-floor room decorated with a more masculine hunt theme, has a queen-size bed, a fireplace, and a smaller bath with a shower.

Priscilla is known for her beautifully prepared and presented breakfasts, served from 8:30 to 9:45 A.M. at individual tables in the formal dining room. They include a cold buffet of fruit, cereal, and muffins plus a hot entrée such as eggs Benedict, eggs Neptune (with smoked salmon and Béarnaise sauce), eggs in a phyllo nest, orange waffles, or French toast soufflé.

The Malones have three daughters (Keely, Briana, and

Erin) and run a stained-glass studio on the bottom floor of their home. They have completed many commissions for religious windows for churches and synagogues as well as windows for private homes.

Closed in January. Five rooms and one suite. May through October, $185–$350; November through April, $135–$295. Breakfast included. Children over 14 welcome. Rooms are double occupancy only. No smoking. No pets. Two-to-three-night weekend minimum. 336 Gibbs Avenue, Newport, RI 02840; (401) 849-1610, (888) ELM-TREE; fax (401) 849-2084; www.elmtreenb.com.

Where to Dine. For casual dining we can't get enough of the lasagna di verdure or the sweet red roasted peppers in oil and garlic at Puerini's (24 Memorial Boulevard; (401) 847-5506). At Scales and Shells (527 Thames Street; (401) 846-FISH) don't miss the lobster fra diavolo. The thick, spicy tomato sauce peppered with clams, mussels, squid, and lobster is served on a bed of linguine and comes to your table in a steaming hot frying pan. For lunch or an afternoon snack get a bowl of thick pasta fagioli with Parmesan cheese and a cappuccino at Ocean Coffee Roaster (22 Washington Square; (401) 846-6060). Creative new American cuisine is best at The Place at Yesterday's (28 Washington Square; (401) 847-0116). The Commodore Room at the Black Pearl on Bannister's Wharf (401) 846-5264) still requires a jacket for men and has an outstanding wine list. White Horse Tavern (Marlborough and Farewell Streets; (401) 849-3600) is where you will dine in the atmosphere of America's oldest tavern, built in 1687. Try the grilled lamb or veal chops.

What to Do. Newport is an area that you can return to time and again. If you choose, you can spend your entire visit indoors touring the mansions. The Breakers is the most opulent. Others along Bellevue Avenue include Marble House, Chateau-sur-Mer, the Elms, Rosecliff, Kingscote, and Belcourt Castle. The 3.5-mile Cliff Walk is one of the most famous in America. On one side is a row of mansions like none other in existence, and on the other the mighty Atlantic pounds the rocky shoreline at your feet. The experience, especially the day after a storm, is unforgettable. You can head to the beach. Drive or bike along 10-mile-long Ocean Drive and see more mansions, grand estates, and dramatic ocean views. Stop at Hammersmith Farm to see Jacqueline Bouvier Kennedy Onassis's childhood bedroom and the office that President John F. Kennedy used as his summer home away from Washington. Go to the 1759 Touro Synagogue, the first in the colonies. Go antiquing, gallery hopping, and shopping. Take a harbor cruise or rent a sailboat. Or you can simply plop yourself down near the water, watch the waves, and take the time to enjoy a good book.

How to Get There   From Boston, take I-93 south, then Route 24 south to Route 114 south to Newport. Turn left on Gibbs Avenue. From New York City, take I-95 north to Route 138 east. After you cross the bridge follow signs to the center of Newport. Turn left on Memorial Drive and left on Gibbs Avenue.

Mari Einstein

Manor House

Manor House, *Norfolk, Connecticut*

In 1898, Louis Tiffany installed twenty stained-glass windows in this handsome Victorian Tudor-style home set on 5 acres in the quiet town of Norfolk, in northwestern Connecticut. Thanks to his generosity, today you can sit at the breakfast table or by the fireplace and admire the shades of blue, yellow, and green shell-and fleur-de-lis-patterned windows.

Innkeepers Diane and Hank Tremblay have created a casual yet elegant atmosphere in their sizable home. The grand living room is dominated by a mammoth raised fireplace that is decorated with a bas-relief of a figure driving a chariot and horses and is surrounded by sofas and easy chairs that invite you to spend hours reading or listening to selections from the Tremblays' extensive collection of compact discs. A grand piano sits ready for an impromptu concert. There is a library room filled to overflowing with books, a porch room, and picnic-perfect grounds that include a 600-foot-long stone wall, professionally designed perennial borders, beehives, and a raspberry patch.

The Victorian Room, about thirty by fifteen feet, has a gas fireplace that you can see from the king-size bed as well as from the double whirlpool tub that's located in the bedroom. The large skylight over the tub, great for stargazing, is an added romantic feature of this room.

The equally large Spofford Room has windows on three sides draped with lacy curtains. A king-size bed with an old lace canopy fills one end of the room; a wood-burning fireplace and chairs fill the other. An outside deck overlooking the grounds is an ideal spot for a private breakfast.

The oversize English Room is a combination bedroom (with a king-size bed and a gas fireplace) and bath (the facilities are located within the bedroom) with a double whirlpool tub and a separate shower.

The Country French Room, on the third floor, has an antique French queen-size bed and a gas fireplace. The large bath with cedar walls and ceiling includes a soaking tub big enough for two. The Chalet Suite, also on the third floor, has an antique French queen-size bed and a sitting room with a small gas fireplace and a daybed.

The Lincoln Room, although one of the smallest accommodations has a wood-burning fireplace and a good view of the grounds (which are pastel soft with apple blossoms in spring). It has a double antique sleigh bed with elaborate carvings and a white fainting couch.

The Balcony Room is among the smaller rooms but it is a good choice for the summer, as it has a private deck. There is a wood-paneled elevator (added to the house in 1931 and still in good running order) to this room.

Guests can have breakfast served to them in their rooms or can join other guests in the dining room. Breakfast includes a choice of two entrées such as orange waffles, poached eggs with lemon butter and chive sauce on English muffins, and blueberry pancakes. During breakfast we enjoyed both the honey and Hank's detailed explanation of beekeeping.

Nine rooms, each with private bath. $125–$250 Full breakfast included. Two-night minimum stay on weekends. Children over 8 welcome. Third person in room $20 additional. No pets. No smoking. 69 Maple Avenue, Norfolk, CT 06058; (860) 542-5690; fax (860) 542-5690; www.manorhouse-norfolk.com.

Where to Dine.   For local dining you can get a good meal at the Norfolk Pub (860) 542-5716) or at Greenwoods Market and Café (860) 542-1551). For elegant dining in a historic colonial atmosphere go to the Inn on the Green, in nearby Marlborough, Massachusetts (413) 229-3131), for a totally candlelit dinner. The Creole spice shrimp, grilled baby chicken, and loin of veal with braised mustard greens and wild mushrooms are favorites. The Cannery, in Canaan (85 Main Street, Route 44; (860) 824-7333), is a chef-operated bistro-style restaurant specializing in contemporary cooking. It features appetizers such as grilled portabello mushrooms with Stilton cheese or arugula salad with pine nuts and pancetta. Entrées include eggplant, walnut, and caramelized onion ravioli; pistachio and black pepper crusted salmon; and sautéed pork medallions with ancho chili sauce and black bean cakes. Julie's New American Sea Grill at the White Hart Inn, in Salisbury (860) 435-0030), specializes in seafood such as pan-seared peppercorn-encrusted loin of tuna or sautéed sea scallops served on fresh garlic tagliatelle. Under Mountain Inn (482 Under Mountain Road, Route 41, Salisbury; (860) 435-0242) serves excellent British food such as steak-and-kidney pie or fish and chips as good as or better than what you can get in London. The Gilson Café and Cinema, in Winsted (Route 44; (860) 379-5108), is a restored Art Deco theater with little café tables that allow you to watch a movie while enjoying a light supper of seafood-stuffed pita bread, a bowl of chili, or beef stew.

What to Do.   For total relaxation plan for a massage with a therapist who lives in Norfolk and is trained to give Swedish, acupressure, sports, or deep muscle massages. The horse-and-carriage livery service in Norfolk is popular with the inn's guests. How about a romantic carriage ride for two? Within walking distance in the village of Norfolk, visit the Artisan's Guild and Joe Stannard Antiques. The 70-acre estate where the Yale Music School has its summer music institute and presents the Norfolk Chamber Music Festival in July is also in Norfolk. Forty-five minutes to the north is Tanglewood, where the Boston Symphony performs for thousands in July and August. Hillside Gardens, in Norfolk, is one of the finest perennial gardens in the United States. The area is full of antiques shops and old bookstores. North of Norfolk is the old buggy whip factory, now home to thirty-eight antiques dealers. West Cornwall has a beautiful one-lane covered bridge over the Housatonic River. Barbara Farnsworth's store has some 50,000 old books. Ian Ingersoll is one of the best handcrafted furniture makers in New England, with Shaker reproductions as his specialty.

How to Get There.   From New York, take I-84 east to Waterbury, Connecticut, and head north on Route 8. At Winsted take Route 44 west to Norfolk. From Massachusetts, take the Massachusetts Turnpike (I-90) to the exit for Route 7 south to Canaan. Then go east on Route 44 to Norfolk.

Greenwoods Gate

Greenwoods Gate, *Norfolk, Connecticut*

You will be pampered to perfection by owner/innkeeper George Schumaker, a former executive with the Hilton Corporation, at this deluxe little bed-and-breakfast inn. The building, an attractive eighteenth-century structure featuring gray clapboards, black shutters, and twelve-over-twelve sash windows, is located .5 mile east of the village green and is filled with antiques and collectibles. Common space for guests centers around the elegantly appointed but comfortable grand parlor, which has an original Federal fireplace—perfect for an afternoon or evening of reading by the fire. If your getaway requires you to stay in touch with the office or to do a little work it's not a problem here, George has added a small computer room off the parlor that includes a computer, fax, and printer for the guests' use.

The Levi Thompson Suite, on the first floor of the house, is especially popular with honeymooners. The suite is on three levels. The luxurious bath has a double whirlpool tub. The sitting area of the suite, up a couple of steps, has a love seat and easy chair. The sleeping area, up a few more steps but in the same room, has a queen-size canopy bed with a Battenberg lace spread. Be sure to notice the well-polished cherry wood floors and railings, which give this room a warm feel. The newly built Lillian Rose Suite includes two bedrooms and a separate living room. (You can take one or both bedrooms.) The Rose Room, the more romantic of the two bedrooms, has a brass queen-size canopy bed. The Lillian Room has a country decor with twin canopy beds covered with quilts. The comfortable library has a simulated electric fireplace and George's personal mementos, including a Chicago Bears football, a Stan Musial baseball, and a Lionel train set.

The E. J. Trescott Suite has a feminine feel, with a white linen spread and lots of lace pillows on the brass-and-iron queen-size bed and an antique dollhouse. The adjoining small sitting room has a fainting couch and a desk. The bath has a clawfoot tub and shower. The Captain Phelps Room has two double beds, a long down-filled couch, and a large bay window with a view of the hills, the best view of any room. The bath is large with a six-foot soaking tub and a separate shower. If you are traveling with three people you can also rent the small Lucy Phelps Room, which has a twin bed and shares a bath with the Captain Phelps Room. Details are what make this inn special: robes; complimentary bottles of Bristol Cream and cognac in each room; decorative touches in each room that are changed four times a year; baths with large bottles of perfumes, soaps, and shampoos so guests can try out different scents and toiletries; and for a bit of whimsy a teddy bear on the bed and a rubber ducky for the bath.

Cookies and tea are out for check-in. From 5:30 to 7:30 P.M. white wine, cheese, and crackers are served. In the morning, the coffee is ready early. At 8:30 A.M. George puts pastry, juice, cereal, yogurt, and fruit compote in the center hall library. Guests can take this "heart starter" breakfast outside, to their rooms, or into the parlor. A hot breakfast (seatings are at 9 and 10:15 A.M. if the house is full) is served in the dining room, which has a wood-burning fireplace and a lace-covered table set with silver and crystal. Frequently served main courses include featherbed egg Espagnol, made with sun-dried tomatoes, vegetables, and cheese; and cranberry, apple, or raspberry baked puff pancakes.

Four suites, each with private bath. $175–$245. 10% off mid-week November through May. Breakfast and afternoon refreshment included. Children over 12 welcome. Third person $75. No smoking. No pets. No credit cards. Two-night weekend minimum. 105 Greenwoods Road East (Route 44), Norfolk, CT 06058; (860) 542-5439; fax (860) 542-5897; www.greenwoodsgate.com.

Where to Dine.   For local dining in Norfolk you can get a good meal at the Norfolk Pub (860) 542-5716, which has a selection of over 100 beers, or at Greenwoods Market and Café. For elegant dining in a historic colonial atmosphere go to the Old Inn on the Green in nearby Marlborough, Massachusetts (800) 286-3139), for a totally candlelit dinner in an eighteenth-century inn. The Cannery Café, in Canaan (860) 824-7333), is a bistro-style restaurant specializing in contemporary cooking. The American Grill at the White Hart Inn, in Salisbury (860) 435-0835), specializes in seafood. The Gilson Café and Cinema, in Winsted (860) 379-5108), is a restored Art Deco theater with little café tables that allow you to watch a movie while enjoying a light supper.

What to Do.   For total relaxation plan for a massage with a therapist who lives in Norfolk and is trained to give Swedish, acupressure, sports, or deep muscle massages. How about a romantic carriage ride for two? Yale Music School has its summer institute and presents the Norfolk Chamber Music Festival here in July. Hillside Gardens in Norfolk is one of the finest perennial gardens in the United States. Forty-five minutes to the north is Tanglewood, where the Boston Symphony performs during July and August. North of Norfolk is the old buggy whip factory, now home to thirty-eight antiques dealers. West Cornwall has a one-lane covered bridge over the Housatonic River. Litchfield is one of the finest examples of a late-eighteenth-century town. New Preston has a number of upscale antiques stores.

How to Get There.   From New York, take I-84 east to Waterbury, Connecticut, and head north on Route 8. At Winsted take Route 44 west to Norfolk. From Massachusetts, take the Massachusetts Turnpike (I-90) to the exit for Route 7 south to Canaan. Then go east on Route 44 to Norfolk.

The Mayflower Inn

The Mayflower Inn, *Washington, Connecticut*

Twenty-eight acres of formal gardens, mountain streams, specimen trees, and 100-year-old rhododendrons form the backdrop to this exquisite country house hotel. As you walk the grounds and through the common rooms you will sense the high standards and good taste of the owners, Adriana and Robert Mnuchin. Since the original 1920 Mayflower Inn was in poor repair, the Mnuchins rebuilt it on the same site and added two additional guest houses, a conference center, a tennis court, a swimming pool, and a fitness center.

The new inn opened in 1992, but the combination of antiques throughout the common rooms, Oriental rugs, walnut and mahogany paneling, fine oil paintings, and decorative pieces lends the patina of age. We particularly liked the richly paneled library, furnished with a fireplace, a leather sofa and chairs, a window seat, and shelves of artfully arranged books, including many first editions.

Each designer-decorated room is spacious and includes a pair of upholstered easy chairs or a sofa. Most rooms have a king-size carved four-poster bed with a featherbed on top of the mattress and soft 320-thread-count Italian Frette sheets. The oversize baths have mahogany paneling, double marble-topped sinks, glass-enclosed tiled showers, and deep soaking tubs. The price variation among the rooms is naturally reflected by the size, whether there's a balcony, and whether the rooms look onto the flower gardens or the woods. There are fifteen rooms and suites in the main inn and five in each of the other two buildings. There are also a heated swimming pool, a tennis court, and a health center with a full selection of machines, aerobic classes, and two masseurs on staff.

Before dinner, take a stroll through the manicured grounds and the exquisitely furnished common rooms. Then have a drink on the grand white-wicker-filled porch that wraps around two sides of the main building.

In warm weather you can dine on the outdoor terrace overlooking the Shakespearean garden. The three elegant dining rooms have widely spaced tables where your conversation is not likely to be easily overheard. Tables are set with Irish linen and French Limoges china that was designed for the inn. Nineteenth-century oil paintings decorate the walls of the dining room and are found throughout the inn.

Service is friendly, attentive but not fussy. Starters from a recent menu included bouillabaisse with a garlic rouille, pan-seared diver scallops with parsnip gratin, duck and ginger agnoletti with arugula and sun-dried tomatoes, and crab spring roll.

For a main course choose from a pasta such as farfalle with portabello mushrooms or ricotta ravioli with a tomato-basil sauce. Other entrées included a selection of fish: hoisin-glazed Chilean sea bass with jasmine rice; seared red grouper with cucumber-carrot salad; and grilled swordfish. Meat entrées are locally raised Millbrook venison medallions with honey yams and French beans, New York strip steak with roasted potato cake, roasted free-range chicken, and grilled veal chop with root vegetable risotto. An extensive, reasonably priced wine list is backed with a cellar of more than 7,000 bottles as well as forty wines available by the glass.

Top choices on the dessert menu include a large cookie shell filled with intensely flavored scoops of watermelon, raspberry, and blackberry ices, and a crunchy caramel peach sundae topped with honey crème fraiche.

Lunch features main courses such as Chinese chicken salad; cobb salad; linguine with shrimp, sun-dried tomatoes, and wild mushrooms; grilled tuna; or bacon and blue cheese burger.

Seventeen rooms, $250–$415, and eight suites, $450–$650; each with private bath. Meals are available but are not included. Children over 12 welcome. No pets. Two-night minimum on weekends; three nights on holiday weekends. Lunch daily, 12 to 2:30 P.M., entrées $9–$16. Dinner nightly, 6 to 9 P.M., entrées $18–$32. Route 47, Washington, CT 06793; (860) 868-9466; fax (860) 868-1497.

What to Do.   Drive to Litchfield, one of the finest examples of a late-eighteenth-century New England town with its town green, its tall spired white church, and grand eighteenth- and nineteenth-century homes. Tour the gardens and the garden shop at White Flower Farm. Drive to New Preston and have a look at a dozen or so upscale antiques stores, and drive around beautiful Lake Wararnaug. Canoe or fly-fish the Housatonic River. In Washington Depot, the Mendelson Gallery has shows of the finest collections of bowls, pots, and baskets by contemporary artisans. Have lunch at the Pantry, which is a combination cooking store and gourmet café. In Kent, visit the galleries or the Eric Sloane Museum, featuring the artist's paintings and his early-American tool collection. In Kent Falls State Park, a path follows the 200-foot waterfall. West Cornwall has a beautiful one-lane covered bridge over the Housatonic River. Hillside Gardens, in Norfolk, is one of the finest perennial gardens in the United States.

How to Get There.   From I-84 at Danbury, take Route 202 north beyond New Milford. Take Route 109 east to Washington Depot. Go south on Route 47 to the inn.

The Boulders

The Boulders, *New Preston, Connecticut*

If antiquing is your passion—or if you want to be in the country on a lake—this inn is ideal. It is located in northwest Connecticut, less than a two-hour drive from New York City. Innkeepers Kees and Ulla Adema have redone the eight cottage units, which Ulla calls "guest houses" because they feel like "little houses in the country." These duplex units offer a lot of privacy; each has a private outdoor entrance, is in a wooded area, has a freestanding woodstove or a built-in fireplace, and boasts a private deck with views of the lake. Five of the eight guest house units have whirlpool tubs; four of these are double-size tubs. All of the rooms except those in the main inn have a refrigerator and coffeemaker. All the rooms have phones and are air-conditioned. Gem North and Gem South have the best views of the water as they are the closest. The baths have double whirlpool tubs. In Gem North you can lie in the English pine queen-size bed and see the water. Gem South, with a king-size bed, is a handicap-accessible room. The quietest rooms are Cobble North and Cobble South as their building is set back in the woods. Both of these units have queen-size beds and a second small bedroom with twin beds. In Fieldstone and in Nugget, the smallest of the guest houses, each of the baths has a double-size whirlpool tub.

Each Carriage House room has a wood-burning fireplace. Pebble, a first-floor room with a twelve-foot ceiling and a four-poster queen-size bed, has an airy open feel and is the only room in this building with some views of the water. Carriage 2 is a second-floor room with a double sleigh bed and a sitting area with a love seat and easy chair by the fireplace. A sloped ceiling over the fireplace gives this room a cozier feel. Carriage 1, on the first floor, has a queen-size bed with a more formal feel.

For those who want to be in the center of action, stay in the main inn, which has six rooms. If you want to sit and look at the lake, the North and South Middle Rooms have love seats that face picture windows, window seats and brass queen-size beds. The Northwest Room is a suite with a king-size bed and a view of the water. The Southwest Room has a deck with a lake view. The Southeast Room has a view of the grounds and the waterfall, and a four-poster queen-size bed with a draped gauze canopy at the head of the bed. The Northeast Room, at the back of the inn and with a view of the grounds, has an especially large sitting room with lots of light. Guests should be aware that this room is over the kitchen. Other nice touches at the inn are the plate of cookies that is left in the room and the turndown service.

The inn is across the road from Lake Waramaug, where guests can swim or use the canoe, rowboat, pedal boat, and sailboat from the inn's lakefront property. There is a tennis court and bicycles for guests' use.

A full breakfast with a choice of entrée is included. Guests help themselves to the cold breakfast buffet, which includes fresh squeezed orange juice, pastries made daily at the inn, fresh fruit, and cereals. A selection of hot dishes could include herb omelettes, blueberry pancakes, eggs Benedict, and eggs done any way you like.

For summer dining the almost-circular Lake Room is surrounded by windows and affords lovely views of Lake Waramaug. When the sun goes down or in the winter the intimate dining room with a fireplace and a service bar is also very pleasant. A wall of huge stone boulders and a massive ten-foot stone lintel separate the two rooms. There is also an outdoor terrace overlooking the lake, a popular summer dining spot.

Inn guests can have anything on the menu. For a first course we had small portions of two light entrées: a radicchio leaf filled with scallops, shrimp, and lobster with wild rice, nuts, and currants, and a salad of baby lettuces with chèvre and walnuts. Appetizers on the menu included grilled spiced shrimp on angel-hair pasta; Maryland crab cakes; and smoked salmon, trout, and mackerel.

The large tenderloin stuffed with Roquefort cheese and wrapped in bacon, accompanied by string beans and roasted peppers, was an excellent variation of a classic. Swordfish topped with fruit salsa came perfectly grilled. The veal loin chop coated with rosemary and lemon and placed on a bed of peppers, red onions, and garlic looked excellent. Desserts included white chocolate and mocha mousse in a dark chocolate cup, lemon pie in a light meringue crust, and a dense chocolate truffle torte. The excellent wine cellar includes 400 selections with twenty five wines available by the glass.

Seventeen rooms and suites, each with private bath. $225–

$375 for two. Breakfast and dinner are included. 15% service charge. Bed-and-breakfast rates are $50 less. Dinner daily except Tuesday. Entrées $18–$27. East Shore Road (Route 45), New Preston, CT 06777; (860) 868-0541, (800) 55-BOULDERS; fax (860) 868-1925; www.bouldersinn.com.

What do Do.   Drive to the center of New Preston and have a look at a dozen or so upscale antiques stores, and drive around beautiful Lake Waramaug. In Washington Depot, the Mendelson Gallery has shows of the finest collections of bowls, pots, and baskets by contemporary artisans. Have lunch at the Pantry, which is a combination cooking store and gourmet café. Drive to Litchfield, one of the finest examples of a late-eighteenth-century New England town with its town green, its tall spired white church, and grand eighteenth-and nineteenth-century homes. Tour the gardens and the garden shop at White Flower Farm. In Kent, visit the galleries and the Eric Sloane Museum, featuring the artist's paintings and his early-American tool collection. West Cornwall has a beautiful one-lane covered bridge over the Housatonic River. Drive north to Salisbury, another lovely small New England town, for excellent tea and cake at Chaiwalla Tea Room. Hillside Gardens in Norfolk is one of the finest perennial gardens in the United States.

How to Get There.   From I-84 at Danbury, take exit 7 to Route 7 north to New Milford. Take Route 202 to New Preston. Turn left on Route 45 to the inn.

The Acorn Room at The Inn at National Hall

The Inn at National Hall, *Westport, Connecticut*

This super-deluxe fifteen-room inn was carved out of the second and third floors of a historic 1873 brick building located on the Saugatuck River across the bridge from Westport's upscale shopping district. The inn is owned by international tour operator Arthur Tauck, who spent over five years restoring the rose-colored brick-and-cast-iron building to its original exterior and totally transforming the interior to pure magnificence.

You know you're in for something special when you enter the elevator and find it decorated with a trompe l'oeil library of leather-bound books. Take note of the titles and you'll wish the ride were longer. The lobby and the living room are on

the third floor. A fantasy map-mural above the cherry wain-
scoting has the names of all the people who worked on the
inn shown as oceans, islands, and countries. Large potted
plants, luxurious swag window treatments, comfortable upholstered chairs, a gas fireplace, and a crystal chandelier from
the Savoy Hotel in London that now hangs over the long
boardroom table create a comfortable yet opulent ambience.

The rooms are sumptuous and were each designed with
many touches such as individual stencil work in all the rooms
created by eighteen artists under the direction of a master
stencil artist from England. You'll find seventeenth-and
eighteenth-century English furniture throughout the inn, as
well as lots of rich cherry wood molding, arches, and woodwork. Eleven of the fifteen rooms are king-bedded, all decorated with luxurious custom fabrics, refrigerators stocked
with complementary soft drinks, televisions with VCRs, and
dual-line telephones. The bathrooms are large and deluxe,
with separate showers with glass doors as a well as tubs in all
but the two smallest rooms. The India Room, a corner room
with a high king-size canopy bed, a soaring eighteen-foot-high
ceiling, and long windows overlooking the Saugatuck River,
is our favorite of the two rooms with the best water views. It
is a very ornate room with walls painted to show an Indian
caravan of characters with details accented with gold leaf. The
chintz canopy is a work of art with Indian motifs to complement the walls. The Saugatuck Suite, with a lower ceiling than
on the third floor, is a corner suite and also has a great water
view, a four-poster king-size canopy bed draped with a crown,
and a separate sitting room. The Watermelon Room is a corner room with a king-size canopy bed and an excellent water
view.

The four loft suites have a living room and a deluxe bath
on the lower level and a staircase leading to a sleeping area.
The Turkistan Suite is the most opulent, with a river view, a

living room with an eighteen-foot ceiling, a floor-to-ceiling bookcase, and a curved staircase leading to the loft bedroom with a king-size canopy bed. The Equestrain Suite is on one level and has a marble-tiled bathroom with a whirlpool tub, a living room with a gas fireplace and a kitchenette, and another room with a king-size canopy bed.

A breakfast tray with morning coffee and a newspaper is outside your room when you awake. You have the option of having a breakfast of fresh squeezed orange juice, fresh fruit, baked goods, cereal, yogurt, and sliced meats and cheeses in the drawing room or having it delivered to your room, or you can order a full breakfast the night before to be delivered to your room at the time you specify.

The first floor of the building is given over to the Restaurant at National Hall, which has a spectacular decor. The lights are custom designed to accent each table, the chairs are upholstered in a light green fabric and embroidered with a ribbon pattern, a large glass window behind the bar gives diners a view of the kitchen, and large windows in one of the rooms overlook the river.

The service is impeccable, and the style is sophisticated New York. A special the night we dined was Composition of the Woodlands—five types of wild mushrooms cooked in Marsala and butter, a dish we would make a special trip to have. A half portion of risotto with lobster, crabmeat, and oyster mushrooms was another great starter. We had a thick seared tuna steak served on a bed of Swiss chard with chanterelles, and deliciously moist swordfish garnished with blue potatoes. Other entrées included peanut-and-sesame-crusted calf liver with caramelized onions; ten-spice grilled lamb with roast eggplant, couscous, and pignoli timbale; and roast veal with Swiss-style potatoes. For dessert we had an impressive seven-layer chocolate cake with layers of dark, light, and white chocolate mousse.

Fifteen rooms and suites, each with private bath. $195–$575. Continental breakfast included. Children welcome. No smoking. No pets. Two-night weekend minimum June to November. Westport, CT 06880; (203) 221-1351, (800) NAT-HALL; fax (203) 221-0276. Lunch, Monday through Saturday, entrées $9–$15, and Sunday brunch, 12 to 3 P.M., $27.50 or à la carte. Dinner nightly from 6 P.M., entrées $18–$28. Post Road West, (203) 221-7572.

What to Do.   Walk across the bridge over the Saugatuck River and enjoy the elegant boutique shopping in Westport, one of the more affluent suburbs of New York City. The Westport Country Playhouse is one of the best summer stock theaters in the country. Visit nearby Stew Leonard's, the largest dairy store in the world. There are twenty to thirty antiques shops close by. Compo Beach is just 4 miles away.

How to Get There.   Located in the heart of downtown Westport, on the Saugatuck River, 1.5 miles from I-95 exit 17 or 1.5 miles from Merritt Parkway exit 41.

House of 1833

House of 1833, *Mystic, Connecticut*

This early-nineteenth-century Greek Revival home located on three acres was converted to a five-room bed-and-breakfast in 1994 by Matt and Carol Nolan. It is located in Old Mystic, a five-minute drive from the Mystic Seaport, and is across the road from Clyde's, one of the last steam-powered cider mills. The house is centrally air-conditioned, and beautifully decorated, and the well-landscaped grounds include a pool as well as a newly constructed tennis court. The Nolans have a young son named Alex. They also have an Abyssinian cat named Molly.

The parlor has a formal feel with a pristine white couch, a white Belgian marble fireplace, and a pair of wingback chairs. The Music Room, the other half of the double parlor, has both a pump organ and a grand piano as well as a crystal chandelier.

The house has five guest rooms, four with fireplaces that use duraflame logs and one with a woodstove. The Peach Room, the former library, has an eleven-foot ceiling and is located on the first floor, off the parlor. It is one of our favorites. It has a queen-size peach-colored canopy bed and matching comforter, a fireplace, and a magnificent bathroom with a double whirlpool tub and a huge shower designed so you can use the whirlpool and then step directly into the oversize shower to cool off. We particularly like this room for a summer stay because a doorway leads from the bedroom to a private side porch with pillowed wicker chairs and views of the pool and tennis court.

Along the curved wall of the graceful spiral staircase to the second floor is a full mural of the town as it was in the nineteenth century.

The Veranda Room, on the second floor, is another favorite. This is a particularly spacious room, with a queen-size canopy bed draped with sheer curtains that faces the fireplace. A Lady Slipper tub installed on a platform and facing the fireplace is a most unusual and romantic feature. A pair of celadon-green brocade matching easy chairs sit next to the window on one side of the room, and on the opposite side there's a narrow porch with white wicker chairs overlooking the pool. A large bath includes a hand-painted sink set in an old bureau.

Two other rooms on this floor are the Ivy Room, with a brass queen-size bed and a fireplace, and the Oak Room, a large room but the least expensive, with a queen-size bed, a fireplace, and a large private bath that's across the hall.

The most private room in the house is the third-floor Cupola Room, with a queen-size four-poster cherry rice bed with a canopy draped from the high peaked ceiling with curtain tiebacks. The colors are plum and gold paisley with muted checks. There is a wood-burning stove in this room, as well as a bath with a double whirlpool and a separate shower. Opposite the bed a staircase heads to the cupola, furnished with two chairs and a little table. It is the perfect romantic private spot to have a glass of wine or champagne and watch the sun set.

Breakfast is at 9 A.M., though guests often wander down to the kitchen early to get coffee. The formal dining room has one large table. The first course is a fruit plate and homemade muffins. During the second course, which could be French toast, quiche, or pancakes, Matt plays the piano in the adjoining room.

Facilities include a new Har-Tru tennis court (tennis lessons are available), a swimming pool, and six new eighteen-speed bikes.

Five rooms, each with private bath. Mid-May through mid-November, $115–$225; other times, $95–$165. Breakfast and afternoon refreshment included. Children welcome midweek. No smoking. No pets. Two-night weekend minimum. 72 North Stonington Road, Mystic, CT 06355; (860) 536-6325, (800) FOR-1833; www.visitmystic.com/1833.

Where to Dine.   J. P. Daniels, in an old barn with exposed rafters, has a strong local year-round following (Route 184, Old Mystic; (806) 572-9564). Diners are encouraged to graze the menu as almost all of the entrées can be had as half portions. In Stonington we like Water Street Café (142 Water Street; (806) 535-2122) and the Boatyard Café (194 Water Street; (860) 535-1381), which overlooks the Dodson Boatyard and the water. In Mystic we like Bravo Bravo (20 East Main Street; (860) 536-3228) for northern Italian. Tableside preparations such as beef Wellington or fettuccine Alfredo are a specialty at the Flood Tide Restaurant at the Inn at Mystic (Routes 1 and 27; (860) 536-9604). Abbott's, located on the waterfront in Noank, is the most well known lobster-in-the-rough restaurant on the East Coast (117 Pearl Street; (806)

572-9128). For an open-hearth colonial cooking experience go to Randall's Ordinary (Route 2, North Stonington; (806) 599-4540), where cooks dressed in colonial garb prepare early-American recipes in this 300-year-old tavern. In Westerly, Three Fish Restaurant (37 Main Street; (401) 348-9700) is an informal waterfront restaurant specializing in seafood dishes.

What to Do.   Mystic Seaport is the largest maritime museum of ships, homes, and shops in the United States. Throughout the village knowledgeable staff carry on the activities of a nineteenth-century New England village seaport. Board the historic vessels, including the *Charles W. Morgan* (1841), the last surviving wooden whaling ship. Mystic Marinelife Aquarium has large tanks of fish, one of the largest collections of seals and sea lions in the world on display, as well as a show featuring trained bottlenose dolphins and Beluga whales. Movie buffs will want to visit Mystic Pizza in downtown Mystic, made famous by the 1988 movie of the same name. Go antiquing on Water Street in Stonington. The best ocean beaches are in Watch Hill, Rhode Island, a quiet moneyed Victorian-era beach community. The nearby Foxwoods Casino, on the Mashantucket Pequot Reservation, brings in thousands of people every day to try their luck at the largest casino in North America.

How to Get There.   Take I-95 to exit 90. Go north on Route 27, 1 mile to Old Mystic. Bear Right at the stop sign. The inn is .5 mile down North Stonington Road on the right.

The first floor front parlor at Riverwind

Riverwind, *Deep River, Connecticut*

Riverwind, a jewel of Americana, is located in Deep River, a small town that hugs the banks of the lower Connecticut River. Here, eight rooms, along with eight common living rooms (four with wood-burning fireplaces), provide a luxurious amount of space for guests' use. The parlor has a piano and a fireplace and a large stuffed moose head. The game room is guarded by George, the inn's resident stuffed deer, who watches over the antique checkerboard. The library is filled with books and magazines. A breathtaking twelve-foot stone cooking fireplace dominates the keeping room. Scattered throughout—hanging from rafters, tucked into corners, mounted on walls, and arranged on tables—is a striking collection of authentic American folk art. Of particular note are the dozen or so quilts collected from the hills of Virginia. This romantic inn is owned by Barbara Barlow, who also happens to be the local justice of the peace, and her husband, Bob

Bucknall. It's a perfect place for a small intimate wedding or for renewing your marriage vows.

Each room has its own distinctive personality. Champagne and Roses, the largest room, is named for the complimentary bottle of champagne and the rose patterns on the sheets, the carpets, and decorating the bath. This large room has a queen-size bed, a private porch, and a bath with a deep tub and a separate shower. Zelda's is a cozy dark-colored emerald-green suite. The old brass daybed in the sitting room is covered with a delicate heirloom lace spread and topped with an abundance of equally lacy pillows. A massive carved oak queen-size sleigh bed dominates the small bedroom, and an old stained-glass window glows in the bath. The Willow Room has a seventeenth-century bird's eye maple four-poster double canopy bed and a private porch. The Quilt Room is a large room with two double-size four-poster beds. Hearts and Flowers is decorated in French country style, with a white iron-and-brass queen-size bed and an antique pine armoire. The lower-priced rooms are Barn Rose Room and Smithfield, both with double beds. The least expensive is Havlow, with a queen-size bed and a private hall bath.

Be sure to allow plenty of time to relax at the inn—to sit by one of the fireplaces, play a game of chess, or sit on the porch with a glass of wine or a mug of coffee or hot cider and let the worries of the world slip away.

The country kitchen is picture perfect—dripping with hanging pots, hams, old biscuit barrels, lard cans, tobacco tins, molds, and cooking contraptions of every shape and size. Amid the smells of baking biscuits and wood burning in the fireplace, we sat down to a breakfast spread (served 9 to 10:30 A.M.) of Smithfield ham, homemade piglet-shaped biscuits (served on the weekends), pastries, fruit, and hearty slices of an artichoke casserole.

For total privacy, or if you have younger children, consider the romantic cottage, a two bedroom house located about a mile away from the inn. The first floor has a full kitchen; a washer/dryer; a living room with a wood-burning fireplace, a collection of CDs, and a television; a dining room; and a half bath. The second floor has two small bedrooms, each with a double-size canopy bed; a sitting room with a television; and a bath.

Eight rooms and suites, each with private bath. $105–$185. Full breakfast included. Cottage, $250 for two, $50 additional per person; continental breakfast supplied. Children over 12 welcome in the inn. Third person 50% of room rate additional. No pets. Two-night weekend minimum. 209 Main Street, Deep River, CT 06417; (860) 526-2014; information.com\ct\ riverwind.

Where to Dine.   Restaurant du Village, in Chester (59 Main Street; (860) 526-5301), serves excellent country French cuisine. Try the cassoulet, the duck, or the roast baby chicken. The lemon tart and the chocolate mousse cake are good choices for dessert. For seafood, go to Fiddlers (4 Water Street, Chester; (860) 526-3210). Copper Beech Inn (Main Street, Ivoryton, (860) 767-0330) has a rich lobster bisque and an excellent rack of lamb. Its desserts are legendary. The Griswold Inn, a veritable institution in Essex, is well past its 200th anniversary (48 Main Street; (860) 767-1812). Steve's Centerbrook Grill (18 Main Street, Centerbrook (860) 767-1277) serves creative fare and is a good choice for those times when you want the option of having a lighter meal. The Whistle Stop (108 Main Street, Deep River; (860) 526-4122) is a small, friendly, informal restaurant less than a mile from the inn.

What to Do.   You must reserve ahead for the popular musical productions at the picturesque six-story Victorian Goodspeed Opera House, in East Haddam, where *Man of La Mancha, Shenandoah,* and *Annie* got their starts. Take the little Chester-Hadlyme ferry across the Connecticut River. Visit the Rhennish-style Gillette Castle, perched 200 feet above the river. From the castle, take Joshuatown Road to Route 156 south to Old Lyme for a visit to the Florence Griswold Museum, known for its outstanding collection of American Impressionist paintings. Take a cruise on the Connecticut River; boats leave from Haddam. Take a walk in the 300-acre Canfield Woods, just down the road from Riverwind. Antiquers will enjoy perusing numerous interesting shops along Route 154 between Deep River and Essex. Stroll around the town of Essex and enjoy the many fine homes built by ship captains. Visit Mystic Seaport to see the last remaining wooden whaling ship and to tour this outstanding re-creation of a mid-nineteenth century seaport.

How to Get There. From New York City, take I-95, the Connecticut Turnpike, north to the Route 9 exit at Old Saybrook. Take Route 9 north to exit 4, then Route 154 north to Deep River. From Boston, take I-95 south to Route 9 north, then follow the above directions.

Copper Beech Inn

Copper Beech, *Ivoryton, Connecticut*

The lower Connecticut River Valley is rich in history. The original settlers came in the 1630s and settled along the banks of the river. In the nineteenth century, Ivoryton became a major center for the importation of ivory, which was used to make combs, piano keys, and other objects. This inn was the home of one of the ivory merchants and is graced by an enormous copper beech tree that spreads over the front lawn. There are terraced gardens with well-cared-for perennials and prized dahlias and lilies near the carriage house.

Innkeepers Eldon and Sally Senner added an attractive plant-filled Victorian conservatory to the front of the main building. They display their extensive collection of nineteenth-century botanical and Audubon prints throughout the inn. Showcases at the front entrance and in the second-floor gallery have

seventeenth-to-nineteenth-century underglaze Chinese porcelain that Eldon collected on trips to Asia. Upstairs are four bedrooms furnished with antiques, all with baths that are original
to the house. Our favorite is Room 1, an extremely spacious
room with a blue floor-to-ceiling canopy over the king-size bed,
a chaise longue, a love seat, two bay windows, and a bath with
a tub with a hand-held shower set into an angled corner of the
room. Room 2 has a queen-size bed in the Hitchcock style and
a deep porcelain soaking tub in the large bathroom. Room 4 has
a queen-size canopy bed, and Room 5 has an early-twentieth-
century brass double bed.

The secluded rooms in the renovated carriage house, located behind the main building, offer more privacy. Each
room has access to a deck overlooking a wooded area, wall-
to-wall carpeting, a mahogany or pine queen-size bed, a television, easy chairs or a couch, and a bath with a single
whirlpool tub. The rooms on the second floor are generally
our preference as the exposed beams of the cathedral ceiling give them a more spacious feel. Our top choice is Room
19, on the second floor, and our second choice is Room 10,
on the first floor, these are the two largest rooms in this
building and each has a private deck. All the rooms now
have phones.

A continental breakfast buffet is set out from 8 to 9:30 A.M.
in the side dining room, overlooking the garden. It includes
homemade turnovers and Danish baked fresh each morning,
fruit salad, juice, breads for toasting, and cereals.

The first floor of the main building is an elegant formal
gourmet restaurant. The plant-filled Victorian conservatory is
a great spot for drinks before or after dinner. The menu is
French but with reduction sauces for the most part and classic
picture-perfect presentation. Favorite selections from recent
menus include sliced artichoke bottom, spinach, and goat

cheese wrapped in pastry; grilled jumbo shrimp marinated in sesame oil, ginger, and spices and served on bok choy; and seared fresh duck foie gras with raspberries. Entrées include a popular Napoléon of vegetables served on a grilled risotto cake, roasted loin of venison, and grilled breast of chicken coated with chopped pecans.

The desserts are works of art: chocolate banana cake and dark chocolate praline mousse served in a pastry flower with caramel sauce; layers of toasted almond wafers, fresh raspberries, and honey mousse; and a sampling of cheeses and fruits.

Thirteen rooms, each with private bath $105–$180. Continental breakfast included. Children over 8 welcome. Third person $30. No pets. Two-night weekend minimum. Dinner, Tuesday through Saturday, Sunday from 1 P.M. Entrées $23–$28. 46 Main Street, Ivoryton, CT 06442; (860) 767-0330; fax (860) 767-7840; www.copperbeechinn.com.

What to Do.   You must reserve ahead for the popular musical productions at the picturesque six-story Victorian Goodspeed Opera House in East Haddam, where *Man of La Mancha, Shenandoah*, and *Annie* got their starts. Take the little Chester-Hadlyme ferry across the Connecticut River. Visit the Rhennish-style Gillette Castle, perched 200 feet above the river. From the castle, take Joshuatown Road to Route 156 south to Old Lyme. This is the area where many of America's greatest Impressionist artists lived, worked, and painted. They came from New York City for the light and the changing color of the river, marshes, and trees. Many stayed with Florence Griswold, whose home is now a great museum, known for its outstanding collection of American Impressionist paintings. Stroll around the town of Essex and enjoy the many fine homes built by ship captains. Visit Mystic Seaport to see the last remaining wooden whaling ship and to tour this outstanding re-creation of a mid-nineteenth-century seaport.

How to Get There.   From New York City or Boston, take I-95 to Old Saybrook. Take Route 9 north to exit 3. The inn is on Main Street in Ivoryton, 1.75 miles from the exit.

The Discerning Traveler®, the East Coast's premier travel newsletter is a tightly focused, thoroughly researched 16-24 page newsletter (more like a travel journal) to destinations from Quebec to Key West. The Glicksteins, authors of this guidebook, do all of the research themselves and spend weeks in the field staying at or extensively inspecting each inn, bed and breakfast, hotel or resort; eating at every restaurant; and visiting the sights that they review.

They always include their opinion of the best rooms at each property. Readers get an insiders' view of the area, including the locals' favorite restaurants, the best craft and art galleries, and directions for backroading with places to stop along the way. Special features for subscribers include:

- toll-free number to ask questions about any of the areas covered
- twice-yearly updates on all of the back issues
- 50% reduction on the purchase of all back issues

The annual Romantic Hideaways issue features 12 special places to stay throughout the East. The other five issues published throughout the year cover one destination each. Portions of some of these issues are included in, *The Discerning Traveler's Guide to Romantic Hideaways of New England* and *The Discerning Traveler's Guide to Romantic Hideaways in the Middle Atlantic and Southeastern States,* all published by St Martin's Press.

Send in the postcard inside this book for a free sample issue of the newsletter or a reduced rate on a one-year subscription.

If the postcard is missing call **(800) 673-7834** in the U.S. or **(215) 247-5578** elsewhere for more information about this special offer. The Discerning Traveler, 504 West Mermaid Lane, Philadelphia, PA 19118